The New Economic Paradigm India in the Covid World

The New Economic Paradigm India in the Covid World

Deepali Pant Joshi

GYAN

Published, 2021

Published by

Gyan Publishing House
5, Ansari Road
Daryaganj, New Delhi-110002
Phone: 011-47034999, 9811692060
www.gyanbooks.com
E-mail: books@gyanbooks.com

Printed at: G. Print Process, Delhi.

Cataloging in Publication Data--DK
Courtesy: D.K. Agencies (P) Ltd. <docinfo@dkagencies.com>

Jośī, Dīpāli Panta, author.
The new economic paradigm India in the covid world / Deepali Pant Joshi.
pages cm
ISBN 9788121220095

1. COVID-19 (Disease)--Economic aspects--India. 2. India--Economic policy--2016- I. Title.

LCC HC435.4.J67 2021 | DDC 338.954 23

For my parents
Jagdish Mohan and Chandra Pant

Contents

Preface 9
Introduction 11
Acknowledgements 15

I. The Macroeconomic Outlook of the Post Covid World 21

II. The Indian Economy 33

III. The Atmanirbhar Package and its Discontents 53

IV. Medium and Small Scale Enterprises 69

V. The Indian - Banks 105

VI. Agriculture 149

VII. Digital India and Financial Inclusion 163

VIII. Policy Choices in the Pandemic 191

Index 201

Preface

The starkest image of the Pandemic for Indians has been that of hopeless, hapless migrants walking home in the blistering heat from the maw of the cruel industrial cities which had no place for them. This, for me, brought out sharply all that was so wrong in our society and of the urgent need to find working, immediate, and scalable solutions.

It underlined the absence of social safety nets for the poor and the most vulnerable and again brought to the fore the need for economic growth to be accompanied by equity. I could not remain immune from those images and it set me thinking and led to this book which is an exploration of our current challenges as an Economy, as a nation, and as human beings caught in the vortex of the Pandemic. The eight chapters of this book are an exploration of these themes.

Chapter one discusses the Macroeconomic outlook of the Covid World, Chapter two the strong fundamentals of the Indian Economy despite the buffeting global winds, its inherent strengths, its resilience, and its capacity to rebound to a high economic growth trajectory on the back of structural reforms.

Chapter three is an analysis of the *Atmanirbhar* Package, while in the next few Chapters I discuss areas which need specific and sectoral policy attention such as the Micro Small and Medium Enterprises, the Agriculture Sector, and the Banks which underpin all financial and economic activity and Financial Inclusion Digitisation i.e. what needs to be done to have a more robust and a stronger banking system, one able to meet the challenges of a growing economy. Chapter Seven closes the book with an overview of the policy choices which the policy-makers are confronted with, primarily the twin challenges of meeting the rising aspirations of our people while at the same time ensuring the scalability and sustainability of economic growth.

The Pandemic will have profound changes on our world, on the ways we think and work and live. It may well be a catalysing factor in speeding up the ongoing global movement towards Nationalism, as Nations close ranks and borders, insulating and isolating themselves physically as well as economically. Optimistically, the disruption of global supply chains may reduce our carbon footprint in the short-term, while global quarantines increase the rapidity of the move towards digitization and an Inclusive economic growth paradigm.

The aspirational India of the 1990s has been replaced by an emergent, more aware India that still demands more opportunities, greater freedom of choice, better infrastructure, and higher economic growth, but without compromising on the safety, security, and basic dignity of our most vulnerable citizens.

These are the subjects of immediate concern and contemporary relevance which have led to this book. I humbly hope to address some of the issues which have high priority on the Global and National agenda and it is hoped that this book will serve as a valuable source of reference for Policy-makers, Academics, Bankers, Thinkers and all those who are engaged in the adventure of building the new India.

Introduction

The Covid-19 Pandemic is spreading like a devouring forest fire infecting millions and bringing economic activity to a crashing halt. Buffeted by global winds, the Indian economy is currently passing through a very difficult phase, as the pandemic and the lockdown instituted to contain it are wreaking their devastating effects. The Covid-19 Pandemic represents the most severe and the largest economic shock which India and the world have experienced in recent decades.

Going through the book will help you to understand the problems, the preferred solutions, and the way forward. The book comprises eight chapters. Chapter One discusses the immediate economic shock of the Pandemic, the global outlook, the overall contraction of economic activity and the effect on the Indian Economy. It also discusses the negative outlook of the rating agencies, per their view of the Indian Economy to which they have assigned a negative outlook and rating downgrades have followed. It also discusses the two major trends which will mark the post Covid world; first there will be a turning away from globalisation to a much sharper Nationalism and second the Digital Revolution will gather pace. Mostly it will be every nation for itself. The Second Chapter discusses the Indian Economy and why the dire forecasts of the rating agencies should not be alarming as the fundamentals of the Indian Economy are quite sound and it has the inherent capacity and will to rebound. It discusses India's strengths and how India can best capitalise on them in the difficult years ahead and weather the storm of the predicted global recession while keeping its economic growth story intact despite the global headwinds. Chapter three discusses the economic response to the crisis offered in the shape and form of the *Atma Nirbhar Bharat* stimulus package. The chapter is appropriately titled the Atma Nirbhar package and its discontents as it does not fight shy of discussing where the package falls short, what are its discontents and also offers solutions to remedy these shortfalls in a detailed discussion which follows in Chapter four- the Micro Small and Medium Enterprises sector. The Chapter discusses the importance of the MSME sector, why it is critical for employment and consequently for harnessing the demographic dividend for economic growth and prosperity. The urgent needs of finance, the difficulty it faces in receipt of timely payments and the trade receivable electronic system which if effectively utilised can address this. The book details the TREDS system put in place by the Reserve Bank capacity skill building and other pressing requirements and why these must be met in a time bound manner. Chapter Five discusses the strengths and weaknesses if the Indian Banking System and of the public sector banks on whom the burden of delivery of the benefits schemes, subsidies announced by the Government to cope with the Covid-19 Pandemic rests it also discusses their own challenges with Non Performing Assets. The shortcomings of the CGTSME scheme the Treds system and what the Banks are doing to address these and why it is important for the banks to emerge as robust financial institutions as they will take the economy onto a higher economic trajectory and underpin economic recovery. It also details the many measures of the RBI monetary policy, its overall accommodative stance and the steps the RBI has taken both conventional and unconventional to address the immediate and emerging problems with the promise of being ready to "Do, all it takes" to help and support the Government and the Nation at this critical juncture in its history. Chapter six focuses on the framework for policy reforms taken up and still remaining in the Agriculture sector critical for food security, the constraints facing the agriculture sector with respect to production and productivity. It lays out the blueprint for the long term while addressing immediate concerns and the reforms taken up in the context of the Pandemic. The last and final chapter eight evaluates the pros and cons of our policy choices, should a fiscally expansionary policy be followed, is it wise? in the long term will it lead to further problems, if not what should be done. Should the RBI monetise the fiscal deficit, is there any alternative to so doing. The chapter discusses the optimum Policy choices in each of the areas, explicated the vellieties of the reasons for the growth slowdown and provides a direction and a way forward to assure not only a resumption of accelerating economic growth but also sustainable, scalable regionally more inclusive growth. It also discusses how the Pandemic has accelerated the move to digital India and how the Jan Dhan Aadhar Mobile Trinity has helped in effective targeting to ensure that the benefits of Rs 500 in women held Jan Dhan Accounts and free grain actually percolate to the poor. It also brings out poignantly how the Pandemic will bring about changes in the world order with every Nation looking out for itself, in our individual lives, how we think, how we live our efforts to reduce the carbon footprint to adopt economically sustainable and viable policies protecting the environment from degradation our sea's, our land masses, the air the atmosphere the world moving with greater consciousness of the environmental impact of all our actions as we industrialise and grow back to being strong and super efficient economies.

India has expertise strength resilience and a demographic dividend which effectively harnessed will lead to economic growth with equity and a dream- a vision of boundless Economic Prosperity.

The book explains the steps taken and the steps which need to be taken. It is a very significant and timely book which will have immense relevance for policy-makers, economists, world opinion makers, rating agencies, academics, students and for all those social scientists and thinkers who are concerned with effects of the Pandemic, the changes happening around us and are seeking reassurance for the future of the human race. Let us look to the future with hope and optimism in the certainty that we as a Nation will emerge much stronger from the crisis.

9th July 2020 **Deepali Pant Joshi**

Acknowledgements

I thank my husband Rajeev for bearing up with me while this work claimed me completely.

My children Paritosh and Kunal for their affection and support Sparky for constant companionship and pointing the way to the study on days when I felt too lazy to work.

The blessings of my Parents, Jagdish Mohan and Chandra Pant, my mother-in-law Smt. Lalita Joshi are always with me to them I owe an ineffable debt of gratitude.

I thank my Publishers Gyan Publishing House and finally nothing that I do is possible without the blessings of my Guru Shri Hanumanji whose blessings make all things possible.

**"Ye sab Tap Pratap Raghurai,
Nath na kachu mor Prabhutai"**

"There is a tide in the Affairs of men
Which, taken at the flood leads on to fortune,
Omitted all the voyage of their life
Is bound in shallows and in miseries.
On such a full sea are we now afloat,
And we must take the current when it serves.
Or lose our ventures."

Julius Caesar Act 4, scene 3

Chapter - I

The Macroeconomic Outlook of the Post Covid World

Economies around the world are in a difficult position. These are trying times, and the pandemic which the globe is battling may well push the world into a deep, global economic recession.

As the toll on human lives and healthcare systems grows, the economic damage is already evident and represents the largest economic shock the world has experienced in decades. In this chapter I will describe both the immediate and near-term outlook for the impact of the pandemic and the long-term damage it has dealt to prospects for growth. The baseline forecast envisions a 5.2 percent contraction in global GDP in 2020, using market exchange rate weights—the deepest global recession in decades, despite the extraordinary efforts of governments to counter the downturn with fiscal and monetary policy support. Over the longer horizon, the deep recessions triggered by the pandemic are expected to leave lasting scars through lower investment, an erosion of human capital through lost work and schooling, and fragmentation of global trade and supply linkages.

The Global Pandemic corona virus Covid-19 has changed the world dramatically in ways which were unimaginable just a year ago. As late as December 2019 the major issues confronting the world economy were not fears of an impending world wise recession but of the fall out of US-China Trade war,

1. Delayed Brexit.

2. Oil Market Disruptions
3. Trade Tensions between US and Iran
4. Deleveraging China reducing global demand
5. Climate Change
6. Rising Social Tensions due to growing Economic Inequality

That fear would stalk the land and Covid-19 would have a devastating Impact on World Economic growth was an unknown.

Global Economic Prospects..- Report of the World Bank

The World Bank takes out a report assessing Global Economic Prospects. This focuses on the economic prospects of emerging economies and developing economies on a semi-annual basis January to June. The present report has a grim assessment which points out that COVID-19 will shrink Global GDP by 5.2% in 2020, the worst since World War II and thrice as steep as the global economic recession of 2009. Its prospects are grim for Europe, Central Asia, Latin America and for other countries like India in the developing world which will be impacted by the risk of global spillovers due to heavy reliance on trade, tourism and Capital ties. Its adverse effects will linger much after the crisis has passed. It goes on to say that 60 million people could be tipped into extreme poverty it could result in

Weakened Productivity;
Depressed Investment;
Loss of Human Capital;
Disrupted Global Supply Chains.

World economies are projected to shrink 7 percent. That weakness will spill over to the outlook for emerging markets. Developing economies, which are forecast to contract by 2.5 percent as they cope with their own domestic outbreaks of the virus. This would represent the weakest showing by this group of economies in at least sixty years.

The COVID has had far-reaching consequences beyond the spread of the virus itself and desperate but ineffectual efforts to quarantine it. As the virus has spread around the globe, concerns have shifted from supply-side manufacturing issues to decreased business in the services sector. The pandemic caused the greatest disruption and unimaginable terror almost like the plague with more than a third of the global population at the time being placed in pervasive lockdown.

Economic Disparities Civil Unrest in the USA. The Long March of the Migrants in India, Police Brutality

Another consequence of the Pandemic is that it has brought the growing economic disparities and the fault lines in society into stark and sharp relief. Whether it is the image of migrants beginning their reverse migration on the long road home from the callous city. The poignancy of worn rubber chappals and dry chapatis on a railway track where tired migrants had fallen asleep and were mowed down by an onrushing train or images of police brutality which killed a father and his son in Tamil Nadu or Police Brutality in the United States which led to worldwide protests, and led to the widespread Civil Unrest in the United States and indignation and anger all over the world after the killing of poor and unemployed George Floyd for petty shop lifting. The anger was in the perceived discrimination against black/brown people of colour in the United States and racial discrimination at a point in time when the world is grappling with the worst pandemic it has ever seen.

Hand sanitisers flew off the shelves and a sense of fear gripped the world. These supply shortages are expected to affect a number of sectors due to increased usage of goods to fight the pandemic, panic buying and disruption in global supply chains this poses long term challenges. The June 2020 Global Economic Prospects Report of the World Bank.

ECONOMIC SHOCK: As the health and human toll grows; the economic damage is already evident and represents the largest economic shock the world has experienced in decades.

The June 2020 report describes both the immediate and nearterm outlook for the impact of the pandemic and the long-term damage it has dealt to prospects for growth. The baseline forecast envisions a 5.2 percent contraction in global GDP in 2020, using market exchange rate weights—the deepest global recession in decades, despite the extraordinary efforts of governments to counter the downturn with fiscal and monetary policy support. Over the longer horizon, the deep recessions triggered by the pandemic are expected to leave lasting scars through lower investment, an erosion of human capital through lost work and schooling, and fragmentation of global trade and supply linkages. For emerging market and developing countries, many of which face daunting vulnerabilities, it is critical to strengthen public health systems, address the challenges posed by informality, and implement reforms that will support strong and sustainable growth once the health crisis abates.

Historic contraction of per capita income

Advanced economies have suffered extensive damage to the processes of Trade, Governance, Health, Labour, Global Supply Chains and Technology.

Covid related recession is now inevitable. Nations and other collectives these include governance mechanisms worldwide have announced the development and implementation of programmes for guided economic recovery.

Gender and the Pandemic

Women, who have always borne the double burden of being poor and being women, have been the hardest hit by the Pandemic restrictions on movement have negatively impacted their livelihoods and their ability to make a living and meet their families basic needs. We are living in a very dangerous world and the fragility of economies and civil societies is increasingly coming to the fore. These risks are not just the result of the immediate crisis but had been pent up in the world economy and are now coming to the fore these weaknesses had been presaged by the 2019 report of the United Nations.

2019 Report of the United Nations World Economic Situation and Prospects

The 2019 report of the United Nations World Economic Situation and prospects 2019 had also pointed out the dangers of slowing growth. Evaluating the economic situation and prospects pre-Covid it had stated "While global economic indicators remain largely favourable they do not tell the whole story. The world economic situation and prospects 2019 underscores that behind these numbers, one can discern a buildup in debt from risks that are threatening global growth prospects. More fundamentally the report raises concerns over the sustainability of global growth in the face of rising financial, social and environmental challenges". Antonio Gutteras, UN Secretary General.

UNCTAD

The United Nations Conference on Trade and Development (UNCTAD) has said that International trade is set to plunge by 27% in the second quarter and by 20% for the year as a whole as major sectors, including the automobile and energy sectors have collapsed from the effects of the global pandemic. The Federal Reserve on the 12th of June had an equally grim prognostication. Jerome Powell, the United States Federal Reserve Chairman painted a gloomy picture of the United States Economy in the coming years. It expects a 6.5% contraction in the economy on a year on year basis. Jerome Powell has said that "Economic Recovery will be a long road".

In India, a National lockdown began on the 31st of March 2020 and continued till June albeit with relaxations to contain the spread of Covid-19. This protracted lockdown has resulted in:

1. Severe disruption of Industrial Production and Factory output has shrunk 55.5% upto 12th June 2020 as the lockdown has severely hurt economic activity. It is reported that "The contraction was expected due to the Nationwide lockdown and a pickup in economic activity may take some time due to the near term slump in the Economy. Output has slipped across all sectors, led by manufacturing with discretionary items like consumer spending showing the highest contraction".
2. Break in Consumer Spending is inevitable, if there is a loss of livelihoods incomes are bound to shrink as a result purchasing power will be severely restricted. When there

will be no consumers of products the production of goods and services will be restricted.

3. The Indian economy is forecast to contract sharply.

Standard and Poor's has estimated India's Economic growth potential at 6.5-7%. India needs a reform push this is the medium to long term growth potential. Despite the contraction in GDP the country is an outperformer among its peers. These are unprecedented times and the pace, progress and overall strength of the recovery is all important.

European Central Bank, Christine Lagarde

European Central Bank president Christine Lagarde has warned that the recovery from the corona virus outbreak will be "restrained" as households save instead of spending while some airlines and hotels suffer "irredeemable" damage.

Household savings have soared since the Covid-19 pandemic hit Europe, rising by 214 bn between February and May to strike a record of 7.3 tn, ECB data released on Friday showed.

"The recovery is going to be a complicated matter, I would characterize it as sequential and restrained," said Ms Lagarde at the Northern Light online summit, organized by the European Business Leaders' Convention.

Standard and Poors Expects the Economy to Contract by 5%

"India's economy is in deep trouble. Difficulties in containing the virus, an anemic policy response, and underlying vulnerabilities, especially across the financial sector, are leading us to expect growth to fall by 5 percent this fiscal year before rebounding in 2021," Standard and Poors said in a report.

In its report titled 'Asia-Pacific losses near USD 3 trillion as balance sheet recession looms', projected the region's economy to shrink by 1.3 percent in 2020, but grow by 6.9 percent in 2021.

This implies a loss nearing USD 3 trillion output over these two years.

The Response of the Asia Pacific Region

"Asia-Pacific has shown some success in containing COVID-19 and, by and large, responded with effective macroeconomic policies," said Shaun Roache, chief economist for Asia-Pacific at S&P Global Ratings.

"This can help cushion the blow and provide a bridge to the recovery. The recovery looks set to be weighed down by indebted balance sheets, however."

Saving More and Spending Less will Deepen the Recession

One risk now looming larger is yet another "balance sheet recession" in which at least one important sector of the economy — the government, firms, or households — tries to bolster its weak financial position by saving more, paying down debt, and spending less, S&P said.

"The downturn caused by COVID-19 did not start as a balance-sheet recession but may end up as one," Roache said. "This means less investment, a slower recovery, and a permanent hit to the economy that will last even after a vaccine is found."

The pandemic caused a sudden stop in activity and to prevent a collapse, policymakers, helped by banks, have provided extraordinary financial support to firms and households.

Banks may lend less than they normally would in a recovery to focus on the overhang from the pandemic. Private firms may prefer to stabilize debt rather than ramp up spending on new investments, even though demand is improving.

S&P Global Ratings kept its forecasts for growth in Chinese economy at 1.2 percent and 7.4 percent for 2020 and 2021, respectively.

The economy is healing but private sector confidence remains fragile. If private sector spending does not improve quickly, more stimuli may be unleashed. The consequences will be more damaging than the cure in the years to come.

The Character of the Anticipated Recovery

Will there be a sharp V-shaped recovery? A fall and a sharp rise characterize a V-shaped recovery. Hopes of a V-shaped recovery are fast receding. In a V-shaped recovery spending and production resumes. This would be a quick rebound to normalcy after a sharp fall. But the last few weeks have cast doubt on this estimation, which explains the rapid selloff. If the outbreak extends into summer, that's a significant loss of demand that can't be made up later and supply chains will take longer to repair.

Goldman Sachs

"Uncertainty around the impact the virus is having and will have on business and consumer spending is heightened and explains the dramatic asset volatility in recent weeks," wrote Goldman analysts about US equities on Wednesday. On March 1, Claudio Borio, the Bank of International Settlements' head of the monetary and economic department, said "no one wants to catch a falling knife" since the expectation of a rapid V-shaped recovery appears "grossly unrealistic."

Citigroup Analysts

"V-shape recovery theory has been significantly challenged, as investors correctly entertain the idea of a far more protracted recovery," wrote Citigroup analysts on the global economy in a note on March 5. "The feedback loop between US equities, EM credit and EMFX in this environment is biased to the downside. It is absolutely clear to every single investor that the general end of 2019 Emerging Market/Developed Market growth consensus is not going to materialize."

Head of US Securities Bank of America

What other shapes are there? We have U, L, even W. Many experts are betting on uncertainty as the only certainty at this point as the long-term effects of shutdowns are expected to linger despite monetary and fiscal stimulus. "The trajectory we have penciled in is a deep 'U shape' where the bottom is quite low, flirting with recession levels," said Michelle Meyer, head of US economics for Bank of America

Securities. If the virus spreads unabated to most of the population in the US and the world, as some we could see the dreaded L-shape or a persistent slowdown.

The International Monetary Fund

The IMF sees Covid -Hit India contracting 4.5% in FY21 the IMF has proposed a deeper 4.5% contraction for India in FY 21 than earlier estimated citing a longer lockdown period and a slower than anticipated recovery. The Covid-19 pandemic has had a more negative impact on activity in the first half of 2020 than anticipated, and the recovery is projected to be more gradual than previously forecast. In 2021, global growth is projected at 5.4 percent, the IMF report said.

In the June update - A Crisis Like No Other, An Uncertain Recovery - of its flagship World Economic Outlook (WEO), the IMF has forecast a - 4.9% global growth in 2020, 1.9 percentage points below the April 2020 estimate.

The IMF had forecast a 1.9% growth for India in the April edition of the WEO and 3% contraction for the world.

The Changes to the World Wrought by the Pandemic

Global Economy

Since March 2020, global economic activity has remained in standstill under COVID-19 related lockdowns and social distancing.

1. Among the key advanced economies (AEs), economic activity contracted in the US, Euro area, Japan and the UK in Q1: 2020.
2. Among emerging market economies (EMEs), the Chinese economy went into a pronounced decline.
3. Economic Activity shrank in other EMEs such as Brazil and South Africa.

Global financial markets calmed after a turbulent period in March, and volatility ebbed as swift and large fiscal and monetary policy responses helped to soothe sentiment. Equity markets recovered some lost ground, while government bond yields remained range-bound, although somewhat elevated in some EMEs due to country-specific factors. Portfolio flows to EMEs revived in April and the rush to safe havens eased. With the US dollar weakening, major EME currencies, which had experienced persistent downward pressure, traded with an appreciating bias. Crude oil prices firmed up modestly as oil producing countries (OPEC *plus*) agreed to cut production, and prospects for revival in demand improved on expectations of imminent easing of lockdowns. Gold prices remained elevated on hedging demand. CPI inflation remained subdued across major AEs and EMEs primarily due to a collapse in oil prices and compression in demand amidst lockdowns, while food inflation picked up due to supply disruptions.

Long Term Repercussions

The Pandemic will have severe repercussions. It will change the way we work, work from home will be the new normal (WFH) Bank, enjoy leisure, brick and mortar Bank will be a thing of the past click and portal online banking will replace visits to Bank Branches. We will have severe lay offs and more knowledge workers we will invest a lot but not in steel and plate glass structures but in digital infrastructure and in coping with risk corporate will worry more about containment of Cyber risk and individuals about their mortality. The pandemic compels us to think and reflect on our lives, economic priorities and consumption patterns. The Pandemic has held up a mirror which has also shown us that humans have been on a self destructive path of unsustainable consumption, growth and ecological degradation. This should lead to greater sensitivity to our environmental issues and the legacies we leave for coming generations.

There are two trends which will mark the post-covid world the increase in digitization, and in economic Nationalism as increasingly nations will look inward to produce and to import substitution and powering ahead through domestic consumption as opposed to export dependence.

This long term vision will impact life, work and leisure. The images of migrants trekking on the long and weary road home also point to the need for a social security net for the migrant labour in particular and the poor in general the best poverty programme is an economy growing at a steady clip with firmly reined in Inflation, this is seriously imperiled. This book is largely an exploration of these themes.

Chapter - II

The Indian Economy

Strong Fundamentals Weakening Growth

The Indian Economy has strong fundamentals yet the performance of the economy has not been encouraging. The fundamentals of the economy embrace the most basic macroeconomic indexes such as economic rate 7.0% (17/18), 6.1% (18/19), 4.2% (19-20), Inflation rate and unemployment rate enlarged these would also include International Trade and Debt. The economy has decelerated to 5% Economic growth. This should set all the alarm bells clanging. The Economy had started slowing prior to the global pandemic for a variety of reasons, while the global and domestic macro financial risks played a part in this process the Indian Economy was also hamstrung by its own contradictions, legacy issues, and past problems.

GDP	*2017-18 (7.0%)*	*2018-19(6.1%)*	*2019-20(4.2%)*
Inflation	3.43%	4.54%	3.34%
Unemployment	6.1 %	5.8%	6.70%
Debt	**1615**	**1801.98**	**2009.81**

Legacy Issues of Inherent Weakness in the Indian Economy

Pre Covid Key Drags on Economic Growth were

Global and geopolitical uncertainties and geopolitical developments:-

1. Trade Tensions between the United States and China
2. Whiff of Recessionary winds delayed BREXIT
3. Oil market disruptions due to geopolitical tensions

Issues Tramelling the Indian Economy

These are pervasive and endemic Issues of the Indian Economy which were present even in the Pre Covid Pandemic.

1. Weak financial market Infrastructure.
2. Banks Asset Quality risk. The Banks have been recapitalized by the Government improving their Capital position and resilience however several challenges remain with the Banks. The NBFC sector has betrayed severe weaknesses and nearly half the country still remains unbanked. It will be a long haul before India has a robust financial system which is able to support faster economic growth fully.
3. Corporate risk, frauds and corporate scandals continue to heighten risk perception and dampen domestic sentiment and that of overseas Investors in the Indian Economy.
4. Recent scandals include the collapse of Infrastructure Leasing and Finance Company (ILFS) which defaulted on a series of loans/bonds beginning August 2018 triggering panic and a collapse in the non-bank lending space and imperiling the NBFC sector as a whole.
5. The aviation sector saw the bankruptcy of Jet Airways after Kingfisher Airlines, adding to the woes of the already cash strapped sector. Despite putting Air India on the block, there are no takers for the airline. The pervasive lockdown also put pressure on the airline sector.
6. The entertainment sector saw the failure of Zee TV.
7. The tourism sector the winding down of the travel agency Cox Kings.
8. Bank scams at the Punjab National Bank led by the diamantine Nirav Modi, Mehul Choksi, and the liquor baron Mallya. The failure of Urban Cooperative Bank, the PMC cooperative bank failed in entirety while the failed Private Sector Yes Bank was bailed out by a consortium of banks led by the State Bank of India. All these successive failures held up the mirror to the complete collapse of Corporate Governance and to the absence of adequate Board level leadership

9. Twin Balance Sheet problems the financial sector was hamstrung by high NPAs and not in a position to support economic growth with the balance sheets of corporates weakening simultaneously.
10. Domestic growth deceleration poses a significant risk reflected in slowing consumption and investment demand.
11. There is a significant risk of increased inflationary pressures in the economy heightened uncertainty surrounding the macroeconomic outlook on account of supply chain disruptions and cost push pressures. Headline inflation to may remain elevated in Q2:2020-21, but likely to ease in H2:2020-21, aided by favourable base effects. As regards the outlook for growth, it appears that the real GDP growth for the year 2020-21 as a whole will be negative. The protracted spread of the pandemic, deviations of the monsoon from the forecast of a normal Monsoon and global financial market volatility are the key downside risks GDP figures for the April-June figures revealed a 23.9% contraction relative to a similar period of the previous year.
12. The slowdown in the Construction Sector as a result of the Pandemic has led to loss of jobs and had a severe deleterious impact on the economy
13. The hospitality sector is in serious downturn as travel for work has come down, hotels are empty. There are no conferences and conventions. Hotels are facing a constancy of overheads lights electricity rates, taxes and zero occupancy.
14. The automation sector likewise is juddering to a halt as consumers have put the brakes on new purchases. The purchase of cars and indeed of all luxury items is at a near standstill.

The Indian Economy is seriously becalmed.

Rating Agencies

Moodys Investor Services

Credit Rating Agency Moody's Investor Services downgraded India's sovereign rating to the lowest Investment grade on June 1, 2020.

The rating agency lowered India's Sovereign rating to Baa 3, one notch lower than "Baa 2" changing the outlook from stable to negative. India still remains at Investment Grade. Overseas borrowing will become more expensive, in the post covid era there will be increased market activity as Companies will try to leverage funds from the International Financial Market. The sovereign rating downgrade will impact the rates at which these companies can raise funds and also dampen Investor sentiment for those looking to invest in the Indian Market.

Moodys Negative Outlook an Indictment of Governance

Moodys negative outlook underlines a perception of failure in Governance it states "Governance is material to India's credit profile and a material factor in the down grade."

As India's debt sustainability has never been in doubt and so downgrade appears a little harsh.

Standard and Poors

Standard and Poors has retained India's sovereign rating at BBB- with a stable outlook long term foreign and local currency rating Long term rating at 9 and short term rating at A-3. It has stated that India's Economy is likely to achieve a strong recovery following deep contraction in this fiscal year, it forecasts real GDP growth at 8.5%. The Indian Economy faces stark challenges in the near term, the downsides are

1. Domestic Vulnerabilities
2. Weakening Financial Sector
3. Fragile Labour Market
4. Risks to long term growth outlook have intensified.

Upsides

On the positives:

1. Governments debt sustainability even in the most stressed scenario is sound.
2. Income and growth levels through the process of Economic Recovery will be on the upside.

3. Reforms in and roll back of restrictive labour laws will positively impact the labor market.
4. UP, MP and Rajasthan have amended labour laws through ordnances 12 hour working hour restrictions under the factories act have been removed this is expected to give an impetus to productivity.
5. The Mahatma Gandhi National Rural Employment Guarantee Programme (MNREGA) if properly implemented is in a position to relieve migrant distress to create employment for those at the base of the pyramid as also durable community assets.
6. Rating Agency (S&P) will assign due weight to reforms in agriculture and labour market as well as easing of bad loan stress of banking sector while deciding future rating action going forward.

Standard and Poors S&P Director and analyst Sovereign and IPF ratings APAC Andrew Wood also said that

1. The reversion to the Insolvency provisions under the Insolvency and Bankruptcy Code (IBC) which has been suspended for at least six months.
2. Stronger regulatory frameworks would be critical in improving the health of Indian Banks.
3. The reforms that will give credence to our structural reforms are those in Agriculture sector domestic markets.
4. These have been introduced and would help address the bottlenecks that have cropped up in the past to make the agriculture sector more efficient.
5. There is a need for due emphasis on the need to create jobs in the manufacturing sector.

S&P for the 13th consecutive year in a row had retained India's rating at lowest Investment grade BBB on their perception that risks to India's long term growth rate are rising, ongoing economic reforms if executed well should keep the country ahead of its peers.

Rating Agencies

Interestingly the concept of credit rating originated in the United States in 1909 when the founder of Moody's Investor Service John Moody rated the US Rail Road Bonds. After the Great Depression where Investors lost their fortunes rating agencies gained increasing popularity. Lack of symmetric information and high costs of collecting information made the role of credit rating agencies increasingly important.

Fitch lowers India's outlook to negative from stable

Fitch has lowered the outlook on India foreign currency Issuer Default Rating IDR to negative from stable but affirmed the rating at the lowest investment grade of BBB- Fitch ratings expects economic outlook to contract by 5% in the Fiscal Year ended March 2021(Fy 21) before increasing to 9.5% in Fy 22. This is a direct result of the severe lockdown imposed from March 25th, 2020. This revision of the outlook to negative was effected on June 18th 2020.

The Fitch moves comes after Standard and Poor's retained the outlook on India to at BBB- while Moody's Investor Services downgraded the ratings from Baa3 from Baa2, with no change in the outlook.

Credit Risk Evaluation

Credit rating is the assessment of a borrower's credit quality. Credit rating performs the function of credit risk evaluation reflecting the borrower's ability to repay the debt as per the terms of issue. These ratings assume importance when there is a need for Indian firms to raise money abroad as the interest rate environment abroad is more benign or for the country to raise funds in a bind.

Clientele

Credit rating agencies now undertake financial analysis and assessment of Sovereign Governments, Institutions, Individuals and financial products.

Methodology

Broadly ratings are based on an in-depth analysis of the Industry and the evaluation of the strengths and weaknesses of the Company. The analytical framework for rating consists of the following four broad areas, business analysis, financial analysis, management evaluation and fundamental analysis.

For whom is rating most relevant, Rating agencies MFIs Banks Investors, rating is useful for all players.

MOODYS NEGATIVE OUTLOOK the rationale advanced was a critique of the lack of improvement in business facilitation

1. Lack of enough reforms to boost private investment
2. Poor implementation of stated policies
3. Stress in the financial sector
4. An inability to control Government spending leading to rising deficits and debts.

Moody's downgrade is linked to the absence of effective structural reforms. That is one area we need to address as it is essential to improving the ease of doing business. The recovery its pace and speed will help tide over the present stasis and may increase the pace of reforms.

The view of the RBI

RBI also does not see an immediate economic recovery and remains cautious on the unfolding economic situation. The RBI view is conservative (Monetary Policy Committee, minutes and RBI Annual Report) states

Domestic Economy

Domestic economic activity has been impacted severely by the lockdown which has extended over the past five months. High frequency indicators point to a collapse in demand beginning March 2020 across both urban and rural segments.

(a) Electricity consumption has plunged

(b) Investment activity suffered deceleration

(c) Private consumption suffered steep decline

(d) Collapse in capital goods production

(e) Retrenchment in the output of consumer durables and nondurables since March.

(f) High frequency indicators of service sector activity such as passenger and commercial vehicle sales

(g) Domestic air passenger traffic

(h) Foreign tourist arrivals halted.

The Promise of Agriculture

The silver lining was provided by agriculture, with the summer sowing of rice, pulses and oilseeds in the country progressing well, with total area sown under the current *kharif season* up by 43.5 percent so far, and the *rabi* harvest promising to be a bumper harvest as reflected in record procurement.

Inflation

Retail inflation, measured by the consumer price index, moderated for the second consecutive month in March 2020 to 5.8 percent after peaking in January. This was mainly due to food inflation easing from double digits in December 2019 - January 2020. In April, however, supply disruptions took a toll and reversed the softening of food inflation, which surged to 8.6 percent from 7.8 percent in March. Prices of vegetables, cereals, milk, pulses and edible oils and sugar emerged as pressure points. The Inflation outlook shows elevated levels of Inflation seasonally and structurally.

Reserve Bank Accommodative Stance

The Reserve Bank remained in pro-active liquidity management mode, expanding its array of measures, both conventional and unconventional, to attempt to ease faltering economic conditions.

Foreign Currency Inflows

Portfolio flows to EMEs revived in April and the rush to safe havens eased. With the US dollar weakening, major EME currencies, which had experienced persistent downward pressure, traded with an appreciating bias.

Commodities

Crude oil prices firmed up modestly as oil producing countries (OPEC *plus*) agreed to cut production, and prospects for revival in demand improved on expectations of imminent easing of lockdowns. Gold prices remained elevated on hedging demand. CPI inflation remained subdued across major AEs and EMEs primarily due to a collapse in oil prices and compression in demand amidst lockdowns, while food inflation picked up due to supply disruptions.

THE IMF HAS LOWERED INDIAS ECONOMIC FORECAST. The Indian economy is projected to slow down significantly.

In its latest update (June 2020), the IMF has projected global growth at (-) 4.9 percent for 2020, with a steeply negative impact on economic activity in H1 and more gradual recovery than expected earlier. India's growth is projected at (-) 4.5 percent for 2020-21. The projections set out by the OECD on June 10, 2020 present two scenarios– single hit and double hit1 - the latter being one in which a second wave of rapid contagion erupts later in 2020. Global growth is projected at (-) 6.0 percent in the single hit scenario and (-) 7.6 percent in the double hit scenario [India's growth is projected at (-) 3.7 percent and (-) 7.3 per cent, respectively, in 2020-21]. In the Global Economic Prospects, the World Bank has projected the deepest global recession in eight decades in 2020, almost three times as steep as the global recession of 2009, due to the global financial crisis GFC, the present downturn is taking place despite unprecedented policy support extended.

"India's economy is projected to contract by 4.5% following a longer period of lockdown and slower recovery than anticipated in April," the fund said. While the decline in Chinese growth is going to be a contraction of only 1.5% and Chinese economy will grow by 1%.

GDP Forecast (%)	***FY21***	***FY22***
IMF (WEO) June	-4.5	6
IMF WEO April	1.9	7.4
World Bank	-3.2	3.1
OECD	-3.7	7.9

Global output down to -4.9% in 2020 all regions of the world the Global Economy will see contraction for the first time and this will also negatively impact India's Economic growth. Though the innate strength of the Indian Economy will allow it to coast past. The biggest strength is the large population and the demographic dividend of a young working age population this will power domestic consumption. China too lacks this advantage due to its one child policy and Europe is graying, the only issue with the demographic bonus which India enjoys is the need to translate this into a young population which earns income. Jobs have to be created either through skilling or capacity enhancements to unleash their entrepreneurial energies.

Slowing Indian Economy

The Indian Economy is slowing but still struggling along at a snail's pace. We have seen the difficult macroeconomic environment and the buffeting global winds. The Pandemic has had a devastating effect on economies globally and has disrupted global Supply Chains it has left death destruction of economic and trade frameworks and destruction in its wake. The Indian Economy was slowing before the Pandemic.

Grim Scenario

The Pre-Covid economic scenario the Budget was expected to provide stimulus for boost to the economy. The present scenario is grim.

1. The escalation of geopolitical tension impacts the price of oil.
2. Rise in oil price increases the risk of inflation.
3. Escalating oil bill leads to an increase in the fiscal deficit.
4. Revenue collection has slowed reflecting a shortfall of approximately 2.2 trillion.
5. The fiscal deficit target was set at 3.3% this targets is very likely to be breached to settle at much higher rates.
6. There is a synchronized slowdown in the three major economies of the world USA, Europe and China.
7. These exogenous factors do not bode well for a resurgence of exports.

Countries like Vietnam and Bangladesh, leveraging cheap labour have moved in to fill the readymade garment tailoring and export space. Despite enjoying the benefits of cheap labour India has lagged behind unable to take advantage of the opportunity provided by China reorienting its economy domestically and the US-China trade war. US is moving away from Chinese imports. India's protectionist push led it to veer away from the Regional Comprehensive Economic Partnership, fear of cheaper imports, is not a long term solution.

Endogenous factors also point to a slowing Economy. There is a marked slowdown in Agriculture, rural demand is faltering, especially for two wheelers, consumer and retail white goods. The auto sector is in crisis ancillaries have suffered and manufacturing and the small scale industry sector are slowing perceptibly. Construction and real estate sector are in rigor mortis. There are larger systemic issues which the government needs to address. Can or these help? The answer is not really. Though the RBI reduced the interest rates by 135 basis points, the transmission has not taken place and thus it has not had the desired impact of boosting economic growth. There is a rise in the prices of vegetables, milk, eggs, pointing to increasing food inflation. The prospect of further rise in the prices of oil will push the RBI into a further corner. If RBI still cuts the rate, its credibility as an Inflation Targeting Central Bank will be called into question. The rating agencies may also not view the overall economic scenario with confidence this may prompt a rating downgrade which will significantly increase the threat to macroeconomic stability in the medium term. The threat of a rating downgrade also looms if Fiscal pump priming is resorted to. Additional Government borrowings for a fiscal push will crowd out the private sector. There are structural and systemic issues which need to be addressed. Agriculture needs coherent policies the subsidy and MSP led model benefits only a few a broader view is required food security is essential so Agriculture needs to be fixed first. Manufacturing exports and employment growth are imperatives. Schemes and programmes which have outlived their utility are a drain on the exchequer; these should be reviewed and scrapped.

Financial sector issues need urgent attention. The banks NPAs may increase from 8.5% of March 20 to an alarming 14.7% by March 2021 as per RBI estimates in its latest financial stability report. The Banks have to straighten their impaired Balance Sheets in order to be able to meet the needs of a Agriculture, Industry, Trade to support the process of economic growth. Banks both Public and Private sector have serious Governance issues. Private and Public Sector Banks need well diversified Boards which actually lead. A solution for the NBFC sector has to be found, tight credit conditions in the NBFC sector, have led to a substantial weakening of domestic demand. The Budget provided a stimulus for some sectors that will not be the solution what is needed is the will to ensure systemic structural reforms. The global pandemic delivered a body blow to the Economy. Faced with a sudden Black Swan event swift steps needed to be taken.

The RBI moved to support the Government by creating an enabling environment for economic growth which rested on the foundation of a soft interest rate regime and easy liquidity while the government response was Atma Nirbhar package. The RBI measures the efficacy and limitations which need to be discussed more fully. A long term vision and a coherent strategy are needed to inform the governments economic policy response.

The RBI Measures

RBI has taken a positive and very proactive stand.

1. Reduction in the policy repo rate and for maintaining the accommodative stance of monetary policy "as long as necessary" to revive growth, mitigate the impact of COVID-19, while ensuring that inflation remains within the target.
2. RBI has been expanding its array of measures, conventional and unconventional - to augment system-level liquidity, both in rupees and forex, as also to channel liquidity to specific sectors facing funding constraints. These liquidity measures are intended to keep the financial system and financial markets functioning as normally as possible under the circumstances so that financial conditions do not freeze up.
3. In these circumstances and keeping in view decision of the Monetary Policy Committee (MPC) to reduce the policy

repo rate and maintain the accommodative stance of monetary policy provides the opportunity for the RBI to announce certain additional measures against the backdrop of a deteriorating outlook for economic activity. These policy actions complement and strengthen each other in intent and reach and maintain the accommodative stance of the measures announced by the RBI can be broadly delineated under four categories:

(a) Measures to improve the functioning of markets and market participants;
(b) Measures to support exports and imports;
(c) Efforts to further ease financial stress caused by COVID-19 disruptions by providing relief on debt servicing and improving access to working capital; and
(d) Steps to ease financial constraints faced by state governments.

(A) Measures to Improve the Functioning of Markets

Refinancing Facility for Small Industries Development Bank of India (SIDBI)

The RBI had announced a special refinance facility of ₹ 15,000 crore to SIDBI at RBI's policy repo rate for a period of 90 days for onlending/ refinancing. In order to provide greater flexibility to SIDBI, it has been decided to roll over the facility at the end of the 90th day for another period of 90 days.

Investments by Foreign Portfolio Investors (FPIs) under the Voluntary Retention Route (VRR)

Since its introduction, the VRR scheme has evinced strong investor participation, with investments exceeding 90 percent of the limits allotted under the scheme. In view of difficulties expressed by FPIs and their custodians on account of COVID-19 related disruptions in adhering to the condition that at least 75 percent of allotted limits be invested within three months, it has been decided that an additional three months time will be allowed to FPIs to fulfill this requirement.

Export Credit

In order to alleviate genuine difficulties being faced by exporters in their production and realization cycles, it has been decided to increase the maximum permissible period of pre-shipment and post-shipment export credit sanctioned by banks from the existing one year to 15 months, for disbursements made up to July 31.

Liquidity Facility for Exim Bank of India

In order to enable EXIM bank to meet its foreign currency resource requirements, it has been decided to extend a line of credit of ₹ 15,000 crore to the EXIM Bank for a period of 90 days (with rollover up to one year) so as to enable it to avail a US dollar swap facility.

Extension of Time

Extension of time for completion of outward remittances against normal imports (*i.e.* excluding import of gold/diamonds and precious stones/jewellery) into India from six months to twelve months from the date of shipment for such imports made on or before July 31, 2020.

(B) Measures to Ease Financial Stress

The RBI had earlier, on two separate occasions (March 27 and April 17, 2020), announced certain regulatory measures pertaining to:

(a) granting of 3 months moratorium on term loan installments;
(b) deferment of interest for 3 months on working capital facilities;
(c) easing of working capital financing requirements by reducing margins or reassessment of working capital cycle;
(d) exemption from being classified as 'defaulter' in supervisory reporting and reporting to credit information companies;
(e) extension of resolution timelines for stressed assets; and
(f) asset classification standstill by excluding the moratorium period of 3 months, etc. by lending institutions.

In view of the extension of the lockdown and continuing disruptions on account of COVID-19, these

1. Measures were extended by another three months from June 1, 2020 till August 31, 2020 taking the total period of

applicability of the measures to six months (i.e. from March 1, 2020 to August 31, 2020).

2. The lending institutions permitted to restore the margins for working capital to their original levels by March 31, 2021. Similarly, the measures pertaining to reassessment of working capital cycle are to be extended up to March 31, 2021.
3. Additionally, lending institutions have been enabled to convert the accumulated interest on working capital facilities over the total deferment period of 6 months (i.e. March 1, 2020 up to August 31, 2020) into a funded interest term loan which shall be fully repaid during the course of the current financial year, ending March 31, 2021.
4. Keeping in view of the current difficulty in raising resources from capital markets, the group exposure limit of banks has been increased from 25 percent to 30 percent of eligible capital base, for enabling corporates to meet their funding requirements from banks. The increased limit will be applicable up to June 30, 2021.

   May not implement counter-cyclical capital buffer (CCyB) framework, as the review and empirical analysis of CCyB indicators according to which CCyB would be activated as and when the circumstances warranted, and that the decision would normally be pre-announced.

   "Based on, it has been decided that it is not necessary to activate CCyB for a period of one year or earlier, as may be necessary".

   The buffer is a prudential measure to meet the funds ratio of banks during adverse market conditions.

STATE GOVERNMENTS Ways and Means Limit enhancement by 30% Reserve Bank has enhanced state government's short-term liquidity needs. The government has decided to enhance the WMA- a temporary facility to meet revenue mismatches- limits to states and union territories ahead of the recommendations of a committee it constituted for the purpose. "It has been decided to increase WMA limit by 30 percent from the existing limit for all States/UTs to enable the State Governments to tide over the situation arising from the outbreak of the COVID-19 pandemic". The revised limits will come into force with effect from April 1, 2020 and will be valid till September 30, 2020. Reserve Bank had constituted an Advisory Committee to review the Ways and Means limits for State Governments and Union Territories.

Inflation Target

These decisions are in consonance with the objective of achieving the medium-term target for Consumer Price Index (CPI) inflation of 4 percent within a band of $\pm$ 2 per cent, while supporting growth. The RBIs objective was clear to introduce sufficient liquidity to support economic activity and to kick start the processes of economic recovery.

To that end the RBI initiatives to increase system-level liquidity as also to channel liquidity to specific sectors facing funding constraints.

Systemic liquidity remained in abundance, with average daily net absorptions under the Liquidity Adjustment Facility (LAF) increasing to ₹ 5.66 lakh crore in May 2020 (up to May 20) from ₹ 4.75 lakh crore in April. During 2020-21 (up to May 20), 1,20,474 crore was injected through Open Market Operation (OMO) purchases and ₹ 87,891 crore through three targeted Long-term Repo Operation (TLTRO) auctions and one TLTRO 2.0 auction. In order to distribute liquidity more evenly across the yield curve, the Reserve Bank conducted one 'operation twist' auction involving the simultaneous sale and purchase of government securities for 10,000 crore each on April 27, 2020.

Extension of Refinance to Nabard, Sidbi, NHB, and Mutual Funds

Reserve Bank has provided ₹ 22,334 crore as refinance to National Bank for Agriculture and Rural Development (NABARD), Small Industries Development Bank of India (SIDBI) and National Housing Bank (NHB) so far (as on May 21, 2020) and ₹ 2,430 crore to mutual funds through a special liquidity facility (SLF) with a view to easing liquidity constraints and de-stress financial markets. Since

February 6, 2020 the Reserve Bank has announced liquidity augmenting measures of ₹ 9.42 lakh crore (4.6 percent of GDP).

Easing of Domestic Financial Conditions

Reflecting the various liquidity management measures, domestic financial conditions have eased appreciably as reflected in the narrowing of liquidity premium in various market segments commercial banks' investments in commercial yields on government securities, commercial paper (CP), 91-day treasury bills, certificates of deposit (CDs) and corporate bonds have softened. The weighted average lending rates, on fresh rupee loans of commercial banks, reduced by 43 bps in March 2020. Though credit growth remains muted, scheduled paper, bonds, debentures and shares of corporate bodies in this year so far (up to May 8) increased sharply by ₹ 66,757 crore as against a decline of ₹ 8,822 crore during the same period last year. There were net inflows into various schemes of mutual funds in April in contrast to large outflows in March. As there is no off take of credit the Banks are investing in the mutual funds.

External Sector

In the external sector, India's merchandise trade slumped in April 2020, with exports shrinking by 60.3 percent and imports by 58.6 percent (y-o-y), respectively. While imports contracted in all 30 commodity groups in April, exports contracted in 28 out of 30 groups. The trade deficit narrowed in April 2020 - both sequentially and on a year-on-year basis - to its lowest level in 47 months.

Foreign Currency Inflows

On the financing side, net foreign direct investment inflows picked up in March 2020 to US$ 2.9 billion from US$ 0.8 billion a year ago. In 2020-21 so far (till May 18), net Foreign Portfolio Investment (FPI) in equities increased to US$ 1.2 billion from US$ 0.8 billion a year ago. In the debt segment, however, there were portfolio outflows of US$ 3.8 billion during the same period as compared with outflows of US$ 1.4 billion a year ago. By contrast, net investment under the voluntary retention route increased by US$ 0.7 billion during the same period.

Foreign Exchange Reserves

India's foreign exchange reserves have increased by US$ 9.2 billion in 2020-21 so far (up to May 15) to US$ 487.0 billion - equivalent to 12 months of imports.

Outlook for the Indian Economy

1. The inflation outlook is highly uncertain. As supply lines get restored in the coming months with gradual relaxations in the lockdown, the unusual spike in food inflation in April is expected to moderate.
2. The forecast of a normal monsoon also portends well for food inflation.
3. Given the current global demand-supply balance, international crude oil prices are likely to remain low although they may firm up from the recent depressed levels.
4. Soft global prices of metals and other industrial raw materials are likely to keep input costs low for domestic firms.
5. Deficient demand may hold down pressures on core inflation (excluding food and fuel), although persisting supply dislocations impart uncertainty to the near term outlook.
6. Volatility in financial markets could have a bearing on inflation. These factors, combined with favourable base effects, are expected to take effect and pull down headline inflation below target in Q3 and Q4 of 2020-21.
7. Turning to the growth outlook, economic activity other than agriculture is likely to remain depressed in Q1:2020-21 in view of the extended lockdown. Even though the lockdown has been lifted by end-May with some restrictions, economic activity even in Q2 may remain subdued due to social distancing measures and the temporary shortage of labour.
8. Recovery in economic activity is expected to begin in Q3 and gain momentum in Q4 as supply lines are gradually restored to normalcy and demand gradually revives.
9. For the year as a whole, there is still heightened uncertainty about the duration of the pandemic and how long social

distancing measures are likely to remain in place and consequently, downside risks to domestic growth remain significant. On the other hand, upside impulses could be unleashed if the pandemic is contained, and social distancing measures are phased out faster.

10. The macroeconomic impact of the pandemic is turning out to be more severe than initially anticipated, and various sectors of the economy are experiencing acute stress.
11. The impact of the shock has been compounded by the interaction of supply disruptions and demand compression. Beyond the destruction of economic and financial activity, livelihood and health are severely affected.
12. It is necessary to ease financial conditions further. This will facilitate the flow of funds at affordable rates and revive animal spirits.

With the inflation outlook remaining benign as lockdown-related supply disruptions are mended, the policy space to address growth concerns needs to be used now rather than later to support the economy, even while maintaining headroom to back up the revival of activity when it takes hold.

In sum the macroeconomic impact of the pandemic and the lockdown turning out to be more severe than initially anticipated, and various sectors of the economy are experiencing acute stress. The impact of the shock has been compounded by the interaction of supply disruptions and demand compression. Beyond the destruction of economic and financial activity, livelihood and mass migration of suddenly rootless migrants who are were most affected raise serious questions relating to the absence of safety nets, the growing hiatus between India and Bharat, the need for jobs and resettlement and most important for economic activity to restart.

Chapter - III

The Atmanirbhar Package and its Discontents

Let us first consider the salient features of the Governments response to the Pandemic and to the slowing economy, in the form of an economic package which is expected to kick start the stalling Economy by providing it both boost and ballast. The Finance Minister announced the package from 12th to 17th May with a new ideological concept of Atma Nirbhar Bharat underlying it.

The contours of response

A. What is the Atma Nirbhar Package? Let us first understand its contours before we critique it.

Overall Stimulus Provided by the Package

The COVID-19 pandemic has caused significant disruptions to the Indian economy. While the lockdowns will be gradually relaxed, the need of the hour is a carefully designed strategy that

1. Clears the path to recovery and
2. Enables the economy to cope with evolving business conditions in the post-COVID-19 world.

The INR20 trillion package unveiled by the Prime Minister is centered on these two aspects and therefore, is believed to be a well-founded approach to restart the economy in a sustainable way.

Sr. No.	Item		INR cr.	Themes focused on:
1	Tranche 1		5,94,550	MSMEs, NBFCs, DISCOMS, Real estate, EPF contribution and some tax measures
2	Tranche 2		3,10,000	Migrant workers, street vendors, self-employed people, small traders and farmers
3	Tranche 3		1,50,000	Agriculture sector and its allied activities
4	Tranches 4 and 5		48,100	Fourth tranche: Structural reforms across sectors such as coal, minerals, civil aviation, social infrastructure, defense production, power distribution in UTs, space and atomic energy
5	Earlier measures including PMGKP		1,92,800	Fifth tranche: MGNREGS, measures related to health and education, making the environment conducive for ease of doing business, PSU related matters and policies thereof and state government and their resources.
6	RBI measures (Actual)		8,01,603	
		Sub-total	9,94,403	
		Total	20,97,053	

Tranche 1

The first set of measures introduced, as part of the INR 20 trillion package, by the Finance Minister largely focuses on infusing liquidity to address cash flow problems in the wake of the pandemic. These initiatives are essential to helping businesses stay alive as well as to protecting jobs. These measures broadly cover six areas:

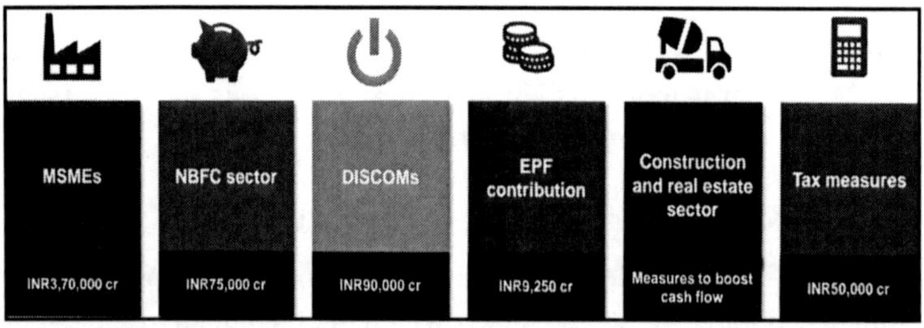

MSME: INR 3 trillion collateral free automatic loan with 100 percent credit cover.

NBFCs: INR 450 billion partial credit guarantee scheme for NBFCs.

DISCOMs: INR 900 billion liquidity infusion to DISCOMs against receivables.

EPF: Statutory PF contribution of both employer and employee will be reduced to 10 percent each from the existing 12 percent for all establishments covered by EPFO for next three months - liquidity relief of INR 6,750 crore.

Real Estate: Relief to contractors by Extension of up to 6 months (without costs to contractor) to be provided by all Central Agencies (like Railways, Ministry of Road, Transport & Highways, Central Public Works Dept, etc.).

Tax Measures: Rates of TDS for non-salaried specified payments and of TCS for specified receipts reduced by 25 percent of existing rates - applicable till 31 March 2021 and several other extensions for filing returns and tax audits.

Tranche 2

Part two of the package announced nine measures related to migrant workers, street vendors, self-employed people, small traders and farmers.

Migrant workers: INR 3,500 crore set aside for free food grains supply for migrant workers.

Mudra Shishu loans: Relief of INR1,500 cr to MUDRA-Shishu loanees.

Street vendors: INR 5,000 crore special credit facility for street vendors, to be launched within a month with an initial working capital up to INR 10,000 to be provided.

Employment generation for Tribals/Adivasis: INR 6,000 crore employment push providing job opportunities for Tribals/Adivasis in a forestation work, forest protection, wildlife protection.

Housing sector: Investment of over INR 70,000 crore expected in the housing sector, which could in turn stimulate demand for steel, cement, transport and other construction materials. Through which Atleast 2.5 lakh middle income families will benefit during 2020-21.

Small and marginal farmers: INR 2 lakh crore credit boost through Kisan Credit Cards.

Tranche 3

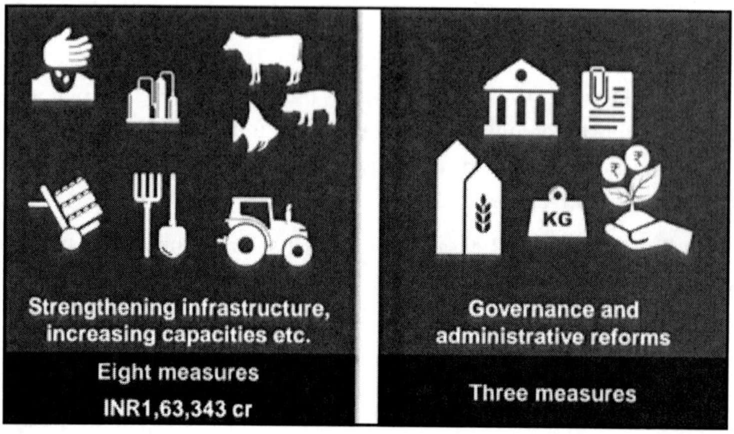

The third tranche of the stimulus package includes eleven measures to strengthen the agriculture sector and its allied activities such as animal husbandry, fisheries, dairy, bee keeping, herbals, food processing etc.

Strengthening infrastructure, increasing capacities: ₹ 1.63 lakh cr to boost infrastructure for farming, micro food enterprises, fishing, Animal disease prevention etc.

Governance and administrative reforms: 3 measures taken which includes Amendments to Essential Commodities Act, Price and quality assurance for Agriculture produce to benefit farmers.

Tranche 4

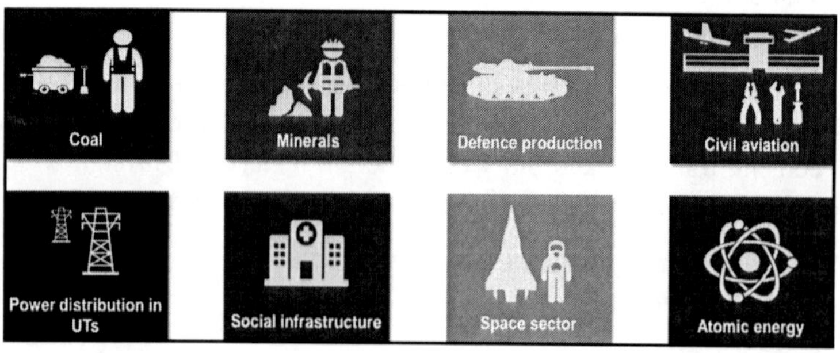

The fourth tranche of the stimulus package focuses on structural reforms across the sectors mentioned below:

Coal: Infrastructure development of INR 50,000 crores for evacuation of enhanced CIL's target of 1 billion tons coal production by 2023-24.

Minerals: 500 mining blocks would be offered through an open and transparent auction process to increase production.

Defence production: FDI limit in the defense manufacturing under automatic route will be raised from 49 percent to 74 percent.

Aviation: Restrictions on utilization of the Indian Air Space to be eased giving a Total benefit of INR 1,000 crore per year for the aviation sector.

Social infrastructure: Total outlay of INR 8,100 crore will be used to boost to private sector investment in social infrastructure projects.

Space: Private sector will be allowed to use ISRO facilities and other relevant assets.

Tranche 5

The final tranche of the stimulus package announced additional allocation under Mahatma Gandhi National Rural Employment Guarantee Scheme MGNREGS and other measures related to health and education, making the environment conducive for ease of doing business, PSU related matters and policies thereof and state government and their resources.

- The Budget estimate for MGNREGA was INR 61,000 crore. The government will now allocate an additional INR 40,000 crore under MGNREGS to provide employment boost.
- Public Expenditure on Health will be increased.
- In terms of Education, PM eVIDYA to be launched immediately. Also, Top 100 universities will be permitted to automatically start online courses by 30th May, 2020.
- As a measure to support state governments, borrowing limits of states increased from 3 percent of gross state

domestic product (GSDP) to 5 percent for 2020-21 only.

- Relaxations in the Indian Bankruptcy Code 2016 and Decriminalization of Company Act defaults to stimulate ease of doing business.

B. Critique

1. Factories are closed; workers are without jobs as a result of the nationwide lockdown announced from 23rd March to mid-June. The images of migrants fleeing the cities on foot, dying like flies, will always remain in our minds. They showed us that there was system no safety net in place for the unorganized workers and the poor migrants and without pay died of poverty, exhaustion, hunger.
2. The effect of stimulus will only impact when the wheels of commerce and industry start moving, if production of goods and services resumes credit can be availed.
3. Contraction for the Indian Economy has been predicted by several analysts. Goldman Sachs contraction estimate of (-) 5% /ICRA Investment Credit Rating Agency of India agrees and Nomura contraction by (-)5.2 %

RBI places economic growth in the negative territory though no numbers are specified. World Bank predicts economic growth of 1.5% to 2%.

Stimulus according to Keynes: Keynes theory of Fiscal Stimulus an injection of Government spending eventually leads to added business activity and even more spending. This theory proposes that spending boosts aggregate output which generates more income. Keynes advocated government spending to kick start the economy typically in periods of recession there will be an increase in private savings and unused resources in the economy.

Increase Government Spending Financed by Government Borrowing Keynes believed that free market Capitalism was inherently unstable his ideas were summed up in the 1936 book "The general theory of Employment Interest and Money" to combat the great depression. The great depression was a severe worldwide economic depression that took place beginning in the United States from 1929 to the late 1930s.

The Keynesian view was that the government had to spend its way out of the recession. Government expenditure **over and above the base level will act as a stimulus.** The series of measures announced by the Finance Minister comprise

1. Already budgeted Expenditure
2. Extension of credit facility with Government Guarantees.

What is the missing piece? There is no committed additional Government Spend. Let us divide the 20.97 lakh crore into two parts

1. Budgeted Expenditure
2. Non Budgeted Expenditure

The BUDGETED Expenditure (95%) comprises LIQUIDITY ENHANCING MEASURES, when is liquidity most required? It is needed when the economy is growing at full throttle. At that time firms need capacity expansion, firms need to leverage bank credit to grow and expand. When there is no economic activity, no input-output, no production of goods no off take of services how will the provision of liquidity lead to an economic stimulus? How will it promote a greater spur to economic activity to revive the flagging economy?

The Liquidity Support is mainly for Banks and NBFCs to jog them along quickening the pace of credit sanction and delivery by banks, the government offers a guarantee in some cases even a 100% guarantee for extension of loans. The CGTSME Credit Guarantee Trust Fund for micro and small enterprises has been in existence for nearly two decades ad has not succeeded. The guarantee cover available under the scheme is to the extent of 50%,75%,80% and 85% even 100% scheme itself has been a failure as the premium under it is far too high costs are uneconomical.

Let's take a look at the Budgeted and the Non-Budgeted part the non-budgeted part is 1% of GDP. Government is relying on the budgeted spending of the National Infrastructure Pipeline is estimated at 12.5% of GDP on an Annual basis. An important dimension of expenditure restructuring would be to frontload infrastructure spending including that on Public Health.

This will generate positive externalities in the form of higher multiplier effects generally co-terminus with capital expenditure and will support Income Employment and Income generation. When services exports took place in a big way in the early nineties, there was a sense that perhaps India had skipped manufacturing as a stage in its industrial development. This was proved as a fallacy in the days to come. Manufacturing is the major generator of employment it cannot be ignored. The Governments Foreign Trade Policy (FTP) recognizes the contribution of Micro Small and Medium Enterprises (MSME) contributes significantly to manufacturing output, employment and exports of the country in terms of value the sector contributes 45% of manufacturing output 40% of total exports and 8% of the GDP of the country. They provide the largest share of employment after Agriculture they are the nurseries for entrepreneurship and Innovation the Medium, Small and Micro enterprises play a vital role in the overall growth of the industrial economy of the country. The challenges faced by MSMEs in India include low rate of IT adoption, the lack of infrastructure, logistics and marketing support, lack of adequate information, improper new product development, Inadequate credit flow, lack of exposure to best management practices in manufacturing and marketing.

Today what economies need most are Security of Jobs, small businesses in lockdown needs support and stimulus as far as possible there should be an effort to ensure that there are no loss of jobs.

Payments in time are essential for restoring the cash flow of cash strapped MSMEs thus firstly their payments should be cleared with immediacy second credit elongation and extension of payments should be enabled.

Advances should be paid to MSME suppliers liquidity is a major issue. MSMEs suffer from scarcity of raw material, finance knowledge skills, capacity building, hand holding.

Credit Guarantee Trust for MSMEs, is a process of triangulation wherein CGTSME becomes an intermediary and guarantees the loan lending comfort to the lender and the borrower CGTSME ensures i.e. guarantees loans upto a certain amount CGTSME guarantees loans to 75 to 80% of loans.

This never took off as the fee structure is considered unviable by the borrower Bank charges an Annual Guarantee fee on the guaranteed amount for the first year and on the outstanding amount for the remaining tenure of the credit facility. Only 8% of MSMEs have availed of Institutional credit through MSMEs, there is a credit guarantee fund for the micro units, but it has not really taken off.

The Trade Receivable Electronic Discounting Scheme

The Trade Receivable Discounting System (TREDS) is a digital platform for accounts receivable. This was initiated as a platform by the RBI in 2014 fill the gap in MSME working capital cycles.

1. It is an online mechanism for facilitating the trade receivable of MSME through multiple financiers.
2. Facilitates the discounting of both invoices and bills of exchange. Electronic discounting it was expected would facilitate faster payments to micro small and medium industries sadly it has not caught on /not worked though the largest PSU SBI and other Public Sector Banks IDBI, Dena Bank and OBC State run firms as Shipping Corporation of India, Kudremukh Iron and BEL, BHEL etc. are on board as its members. (Annex 1 has full details of the Treds scheme)

In this scenario

Support from Government is required to stimulate demand procurement from MSMEs should be increased by Govt. PSUs can list the invoices on Treds any Co over 500 crore is required to be registered discounting of invoices will help create demand and liquidity

1. For supply chains to be restarted in this
2. Stimulate consumer demand

Produce Medical Equipment PPE with a buy back from government.

It is vital to extend Tax Concessions, GST and the impact on accounts receivable discounting of invoices becomes important.

The three critical needs are:

A. Capital, Government can support by releasing payments and releasing Income Taxes.

B. Demand which can also be created by government.
C. Infrastructure is needed like power, electricity, fuel, labour is also required.
D. Efforts and enabling conditions are necessary, to be made to bring back the migrants.
E. There are 51 labour laws so rationalization of labour laws for which an initiative has been taken by states like UP and Maharashtra should be universalized.
F. It is essential to ensure an assessment of regional sectorial industry-wise disparities in credit flow to MSME.
G. Due to the still high rates for CGTSME guarantees and low demand the stressed MSMEs are not able to tap into the relief ostensibly extended by Government through the Banking System.

The Absence of Funding Support for States

Borrowing limits for States have been enhanced to 5% of GSDP from 3% with a caveat of conditionality's. While the borrowing limits are a one time enhancement the conditions subject to which these will be extended will be permanent.

States will have to undertake reforms including "One Nation, One Ration Card" Power distribution reforms and ease of doing business reforms increasing job creation through investment and promoting urban development, health and sanitation. An increase in the States borrowing limits will allow for greater Capital Expenditure despite the plunge in revenue receipts of the additional borrowing firstly this will be in tranches the first 0.5% will unconditional while the next 1% will be in four equal tranches each linked to clearly specified measurable and monitorable reform measures.

This will discourage rather than encourage States to borrow.

Fiscal Deficit

Combined Fiscal Deficit of Centre and States may aggregate 12% of GDP. How will the deficit be bridged if the financial savings of the household sector, savings of Public Sector Banks and net capital inflows are insufficient? The government's fiscal deficit target estimated in the Union Budget 2020-21 was ₹ 7.96 lakh crore, or 3.5 percent of the GDP, but due to the slowdown and covid-19 led lockdown, is likely to be revised due to the impact of the corona virus-led lockdown in the economy. Economists had predicted the figures might go up substantially. This was despite the government announcing various measures including cutting many non-essential expenditure under several heads, suspending announcement of any new scheme till March 30, 2021.

The government has received ₹ 45,498 crore, till the May, which was 2.03 percent of the budget estimate. In the same period, total expenditure incurred was ₹ 5,11,841 crore, which was 16.82 percent of budget estimate, mainly due to many relief measures announced during the pandemic. Tax revenues are also a point of concern. Out of the total receipt, net tax revenue was ₹ 33,850 crore, while non-tax revenue was ₹ 10,817 crore.

Non-debt capital receipts stood at ₹ 831crore on account of recovery of loans. Further, the government said it had transferred ₹ 92,077 crore to the state governments as Devolution of Share of Taxes in this period, which is ₹ 7,010 crore lower than the previous year. Out of the total expenditure, ₹ 4,56,635 crore was on revenue account, including ₹ 78,265 crore on account of interest payments and ₹ 67,469 crore due to major subsidies, while ₹ 55,206 crore was on the capital account.

As the natural pace of spending is expected to be high, coupled with subdued revenue, the government had already increased its borrowing for the current year to ₹ 12 lakh crore against ₹ 7.8 lakh crore budgeted earlier.

Reforms

1. Labour Market reforms these are best executed when an economy is on the upswing and not when it is stalling.
2. Reforms in Agriculture specifically agricultural markets.

Prospects of Economic Recovery

Economic Recovery from the Post-Covid shock is not going to be easy. Policy decisions in the near term will inform the contours i.e., the strength and durability of the recovery.

Atmanirbhar Package Overall Tepid Response

The contours of response do not engender much confidence.

1. No long term strategy vision informs the hastily cobbled together package.
2. The Atmanirbhar Bharat package announced with a great deal of fanfare as 10% of GDP translates to a modest 1.5% of GDP as direct fiscal stimulus increasing to 3.5% of GDP if contingent liabilities are also included.
3. Negative Economic Growth which we are presently faced which requires more spending and more funds for States hence sharply targeted measures backed by adequate funds are required.
4. Though on the face of it the package seems attractive there is no indication of where the generous allocations will be sourced from.
5. The Finance Ministers announcements comprise a mix and match of Previous Announcement by the Prime Minister post Covid-19 but pre the Finance Ministers announcement.
6. It tries to blur the difference between already Budgeted Expenditure and Non Budgeted Expenditure.
7. If we view it through a strict binary lens of budgeted and Non Budgeted expenditure we find that while 85% is budgeted expenditure only the remainder 15% remains.
8. It veers around the semantics of reforms in land, labour laws and Capital.

Fiscal measures are linked to Government Revenue and Government Expenditure, Government Revenue flows from taxes and Expenditure from Government Investments in Infrastructure, Public Health et. al.

Pre the 12th of May the Prime Minister made the following announcements:

Tax Concessions of 7,800

Health Package 15,000 crore for Covid

PM Gareeb Kalyan Yojana 1,52,800 i.e. Direct Benefit transfers for women Jan Dhan account holders and workers and for farmers 500 to 2000 crore free food grains and free travel for migrants.

Impact of the Change in the Definition of the MSMEs

There is a change in the definition for MSMEs. As against Investment in plant and machinery this is now linked to turnover. This is good to the extent that it helps medium enterprises avoid the backwardness trap but if the overall size of the pie remains the same then it further squeezes out the microenterprises medium enterprises will be linked to a turnover of 200 crore, if the services sector is not to be squeezed out completely it is essential for a subtarget to be mandated within these broad and generous turnover limits.

Delivery Challenge is Immense

On June 4th the government made three significant announcements:

1. Amendment to the Essential Commodities Act 1955 which will free the prices of cereals, pulses, oilseeds, edible oils, onions and potatoes from stock limits except in the case of natural calamities like famines.
2. Two allowing farmers to sell their crop to anyone anywhere under current laws they can only sell to licensed traders in APMC Agricultural Produce Marketing Committee Mandis near them.
3. Allowing Contract farming: This will enable farmers to engage with processors, wholesalers, aggregators, large retailers, exporters etc and will also enable them to access Capital and Technology.

The efficacy of ANBA rests on private investment and easy flow of credit to agriculture and MSMEs. It relied on NABARD and SIDBI to roll out the package in good measure as investment and refinance arms in their related domains. Public-private participation holds the key for investments which, depend on the initiatives of SEBI and the stock market movements. Reforms in agriculture, bold in character, announced in ANBA also call for huge investments in digital infrastructure as e-NAM, aggregators, PACs and FPOs. These are the drivers of market reforms. Farmers rejoice and look forward to selling their produce wherever it fetches the price they expect. Price discovery will take a departure from the reliance in MSP. Unheard of and unseen investments will be seen in the farm sector. Stability of growth in farm sector will eventually lead the $5 tn growth of Indian economy.

RBI Governor in a recent address indicated that he would like to look at the priority sector categorisation afresh to ensure that it delivers the intended benefits. This assumes greater importance in financial inclusion agenda as efforts hitherto like Jan Dhan, MUDRA, SME 99-Minute Loans etc could make only numerical and not qualitative advances.

Narrowly Focussed and Nuanced Programmes

Direct credit programmes in Korea, Japan in 1950s and 1980s revealed the need for narrowly focused and nuanced programmes with sunset clauses delivered the results. The problem with directed credit is essentially three-fold: First, pricing at its true market level, second, avoidance of the persons who are not credit-constrained, and third, selection of focused areas and regions without political interference in undefined democracy.

Credit discipline and equity, the twin principles of credit dispensation suffered a systemic failure with unwarranted interventions loan waivers and perverse incentives MSP. Both farm and micro and small enterprises require credit with extension, handholding, monitoring and supervision as key deliverable. This calls for out-of-the-box thinking. Re-engineering the stressed institutions is one challenge while bringing integrity and transparency is the second challenge. 3 tn roll out to the MSMEs with ₹ 25 crore outstanding credit and a turnover of ₹ 100 cr with an incremental 20 percent secured to the extent of default threshold of around 14 per Rupees spent from the guarantee of National Credit Guarantee Trust the progress will require monitoring on the ground. Most MSME surveys reveal that only a few top-end enterprises of the sector will benefit. Micro will be the least beneficiaries. Banks are already competing to be popular in the eyes of the Ministry of Finance (MoF) by rolling out the sanctions under the scheme. There is a gulf between the readily sanctioned loans and the lag with which these sanctions translate to disbursements and a further lag before the units are actually grounded. The announcements are declarations of intent.

Ministry of MSME on its part has done all that it could do: Government e-Market Place (GeM), Government e-Market Place were common user goods and services can be Procured TReDS, real push for digitisation, procurement policy, redefining the sector at the right moment combining investment in plant and machinery and turnover in different proportions, and a new threshold of ₹ 200 crore for tendering process. Any issue relating to MSME - whether related to finance or infrastructure or trade or export, although should be dealt with the respective domains, falls to the lot of the MSME Ministry to resolve and hence takes inordinate time to coordinate and resolve.

Chapter - IV

Medium and Small Scale Enterprises

Critical Importance of MSME's Employment and Entrepreneurship

With 63.4 million units throughout the geographical expanse of the country MSME's contribute 29.7% to GDP around 6.11% of the manufacturing GDP and 24.63% of the GDP from service activities as also 33.4% of India's Manufacturing output and in India, a country of subcontinental proportions with a population size of about 1.3 billion, the Micro, Small and Medium Enterprises (MSME) sector has a vital role in the economy. It fosters entrepreneurship and generates large employment opportunities.

Covid-19 Pandemic Atmanirbhar Scheme and the Banks

A package of measures was announced in May 2020 under Atmanirbhar Bharat Abhiyan in five tranches cover, among others, rural employment generation, infrastructure, MSMEs, NBFCs, migrant workers and ease of doing business. These measures aggregate around 20 lakh crore or 10 percent of GDP and aim to address the difficulties faced by various categories including MSMEs, NBFCs, power distribution companies and infrastructure projects. The measures, both short-term and long-term in nature, also endeavour to make India self-reliant by boosting private participation in numerous sectors with global quality and competitiveness. The growth of India's personal protective equipment (PPE) sector from scratch before March 2020 to making

1,50,000 pieces a day by beginning of May 2020 shows the potential of India in meeting the challenges.

MSMEs in pandemic could benefit from policies

1. Collateral free loan of 3 lakh crore.
2. Subordinate debt provision of 20,000 crore.
3. Equity infusion.
4. The change in definition of classification of MSMEs by including turnover as basis of definition will allow MSMEs to expand without losing benefits and also improve ease of doing business by aligning them with GST.
5. The structural reforms introduced as part of fourth tranche of stimulus is expected to bring in private investments.
6. The proposed change in public sector enterprise policy, where all sectors will be opened to private sectors, and public-sector enterprises will operate only in notified strategic sectors, will bring in far-reaching changes in India's industrial sector.
7. In the manufacturing sector, 100 percent FDI in contract manufacturing and commercial coal mining through the automatic route is expected to bring in more private investments.

   Banks have started disbursing credit to MSMEs under the 100% Emergency Credit Line (3 lakh crore Government Guaranteed under the Emergency Credit Line Guarantee Scheme, ECLGS scheme announced as part of the Atma Nirbhar Bharat (ANB) package. However, for many firms which have taken a hit in the Pandemic lockdown access to credit remains a tremendous challenge. While banks are extending lines of credit to their existing MSME customers as new borrowers do not form part of the constituents of the Atma Nirbhar Package these remain credit constrained.

Double Whammy for Small SME Covid-19 Demand Compression and Credit Constraints

As the size of the pie of credit extended under the Atma Nirbhar programme, remains the same the change in definition arguable allows the larger companies to willy nilly elbow their way in and squeeze out the smaller companies, while completely removing the services and the tiniest units from the scene. Viable companies with good and established credit histories are able to raise funds but the most needy of the MSMEs face a double whammy, slump in demand coupled with lack of funds to kick start operations. As per official data as of June 18th, state owned banks sanctioned loans of 40,416 crores under the scheme of which ₹ 21,02855 crore has been disbursed.

Exclusion of First Time Borrowers

The scheme categorically excluded first time borrowers and those whose accounts have turned bad. A separate scheme for stressed MSMEs has been announced, is in the works, but has not been operationalised as yet, Banks are not seeking fresh collateral on these loans under the scheme, however as it is extended to only existing borrowers already availing credit facilities from banks, their factory, land plant and machinery is mostly pledged with banks.

Rates of Interest

The rate of interest charged by the Banks is almost at par with market rates and does not offer any substantial concessions. In May the RBI cut Repo rates 40 basis points bringing them to a record all time low of 4% This has not translated to any relief for the MSME borrowers as under the scheme interest rates which can be levied by Banks have been capped at 9.25% per annum, while Non Banking Financial Companies can lend at a maximum of 14% per annum. State owned Banks are lending at 8%,depending on the credit worthiness of the borrower.

Stressed Companies Need Working Capital Loans for the Lockdown Period

High rates of interest serve to exclude stressed companies that need a working capital loan for the period that their companies were shut. These loans are very necessary to enable them to defray salaries and ensure that there are no lay offs. Job loss and employment cut backs, are the first defence of small companies facing stress.

Reducing Fixed Costs

MSMEs also need government support for lowering fixed costs and short term benefits like waiver of electricity charges "Otherwise not many will survive this onslaught and will have to wind up." said the President of the Federation of Indian Micro Small and Medium enterprises. SEVERE HIT ON PROFITABILITY CRISIL expects the profitability of MSMEs to fall sharply, hitting micro enterprises the hardest. Micro enterprises account for 32% of the overall MSME debt. Consumer discretionary item manufacturing, construction sectors, Export linked MSMEs, and textile and ceramics players are perceived as the hardest hit.

Employment Opportunities

As MSMEs absorb the surplus agricultural labour, they help reduce the problem of disguised unemployment in rural areas. MSMEs are also complementary to large industries as ancillary units and also play an important role in the whole eco-system of the secondary and tertiary sector. The 73rd round of National Sample Survey (NSS) conducted during the period 2015-16, the estimated employment in MSME sector was around 11 crore. Within MSME sector, each of the three subsectors, namely, trade, manufacturing and other services accounted for about a third of total employment. Around 50 percent of the total MSMEs operate in rural areas and provide 45 percent of total employment.

The Missing Middle

The micro enterprises account for 97 percent of total employment in MSME sector. This relates to the problem of what is called the missing middle which suggests that micro firms have failed to grow into smaller and medium firms and so on over time. This seems to have kept the micro sector bereft of enjoying economies of scale, investment into fixed assets, adoption of technology and innovation.

The Backwardness Trap

As incentives were linked to size in order to avail of the benefits the MSMEs were reluctant to expand by investing in plant and machinery or updating the same. This led to working with outmoded machinery severely impacting their productivity and to the backwardness trap. They do not want to grow for fear of losing state patronage and subsidies and other incentives.

The Need for Technology Upgradation to Enhance Competitiveness

The share of MSME sector in India's merchandise exports stood at around 48 percent in 2018-196. This signifies that Indian MSMEs are becoming globally competitive and their products/services are being accepted overseas. In this background, special attention needs to be given to improve the competitiveness and technology up-gradation endeavours. Various schemes and programmes of the government, therefore, should be continued and effectively implemented.

COVID-19 Adverse Impact

Like other sectors of the Indian economy, MSMEs have been hit badly due to lockdown imposed by the government to tackle Covid-19 pandemic. However, even before the current crisis, MSMEs growth has been marred by several challenges. Considering the importance of MSME sector, Government of India provides guarantee coverage to banks to extend collateral/ third party guarantee free credit facilities to MSE sectors. Further, of the ₹ 20 lakh crore Covid-19 economic package announced the Prime Minister toward Atmanirbhar Bharat Yojna, ₹ 3 lakh crore has been earmarked for collateral free loan schemes for the MSME sector with CGTSME guarantee. Despite all these announcements, collateral free loan schemes with CGTMSE coverage has not been a favourite among bankers.

Critique

In such a critical situation, caused by the Covid-19 pandemic providing merely a stimulus package may not be effective, until adequate reforms are carried out to solve MSME pressing problems and to utilise its sectoral potential.

Credit Woes

- The biggest problem is of credit. Finance in adequate

quantum as required and at the right time, without delay is sorely needed by the MSMEs. Is credit guarantee a solution? It is merely a small and not very effective sop partially a solution.

Challenges Faced by Banks While Extending Loans to MSMEs with CGTSME Coverage

The challenges before the banks while extending loans to MSE sector with CGTMSE. Despite the loans secured by collaterals, banks find it difficult to recover full amount because of the deterioration in economic conditions due to the Covid-19 Pandemic and subsequent erosion in collateral values. Higher NPA weakens the balance sheets of banks and banks will have to pump additional capital which is a great challenge in meeting the targets under the Atma Nirbhar Programme.

Reason for Giving Credit Guarantees

- A credit guarantee by the government helps as it assures the bank that its loan will be repaid by the government in case the MSME falters.
- Efforts to pump liquidity via the bank have not been successful in the past, because banks simply do not want to lend any new money.
- Banks, quite justifiably, suspect that any new loans will only add to their growing mountain of non-performing assets.
- So the issue was banks had the money but were not willing to lend to the credit-starved sections of the economy.
- Thus, as part of the solution, credit guarantees are chosen by the government.

Significance of MSMEs

- The significance of the MSMEs sector can be noted from the fact that it is the second-largest employment provider, after agriculture in India.
- In India, at present, there are nearly 56 million such enterprises in various industries, employing close to 124 million people.

- Of these, nearly 14% are women-led enterprises, and close to 60% are based in rural areas.

- In all, the MSME sector accounts for 8% of India's GDP and 45% of merchandise exports.
- Due to this, the MSME sector is called the growth engine of the nation.

Challenges Pertaining to MSMEs

Lack of Adequate and Timely Access to Finance

- Access to finance continues to remain the biggest challenge for MSMEs and has constrained their growth.
- MSME funding from banks has been stalled, as decision-making managers are reluctant of loans going bad.
- As Banks were reluctant to lend the MSMEs turned to the Non Bank Finance Sector and to the urban cooperative banks. The sudden winding down of ILFS and the equally dramatic folding up of the Punjab and Maharashtra Cooperative Bank and the domino effect on other Urban Cooperative Banks and its effect on the other NBFCs (Non-Banking Finance Companies led to a severe funds crunch as UCBs and NBFCs gre wary of fresh lending and rushed to make adequate provision for the existing loans on their balance sheets while cutting back on new loans. MSMEs ran into deep trouble because of the liquidity crunch that followed.
- Due to this, MSMEs are not able to invest in manufacturing, purchase raw materials on time, access new technologies or acquire new skills due to lack of funds which is a big handicap especially in its fight with global competitors.

Technological Disruption

- India's MSME sector is based on obsolete technology, which hampers its production efficiency.
- With the emergence of new technologies like Artificial Intelligence, Data Analytics, Robotics and related technologies is a bigger challenge for MSMEs than for organized large

scale manufacturing as they lack the financial strength for upgradation.

Red Tape

- MSMEs require a lot of government services and approvals, for which the entrepreneur has to run around various government departments.
  - Getting construction permits, enforcing contracts, paying taxes, starting a business and trading across borders continue to constrain doing business.
- Regulatory risks and policy uncertainty in the past have dented investor confidence.

Problem of Scale

- Majority of the firms in MSMEs are micro-enterprises.
- The MSME space is virtually a micro space formed by a plethora of small and local shops and hence, scaling them up is a problem, especially when fund access is challenging.

Steps to be Initiated

- **Increasing Domestic Manufacturing Capabilities:** The government can play a crucial role in creating domestic manufacturing capabilities by leveraging proposed public procurement and projects.
  - For example, Mega public projects such as Sagarmala, Bharatmala, industrial corridors, and the Pradhan Mantri Awas Yojana (PMAY) can stimulate domestic manufacturing activities.
  - This should be accompanied by a simplification of the regulatory process.
- Cluster Manufacturing: Efforts should be made to develop self-sufficient clusters of manufacturing competence, with Cluster Administrative Authorities, empowered to provide single window clearances to entrepreneurs and investors.
- Leveraging Industrial Revolution 4.0: Disruptive technology, while leading to job losses in traditional areas, also presents new job opportunities.

- A greater connect between government-industry-academia is required to identify the changing requirements in manufacturing and prepare an employable workforce.
- Also, the Industrial Revolution 4.0 will boost the Industrial supply chains in India.

- **Need to improve Ease of Doing business:** Reforms: India has already taken several steps, due to which ease of doing business in India has improved significantly (India's ranking in has improved from 142 in 2014 to 63 in 2020).
    - However, still some reforms are needed in regard, especially in the field of land, labour reforms and in enforcing contracts.
- **Making Indian Products to Match Global Standards:** There is a need for harmonizing Indian quality standards with global standards in many sectors.
    - Lack of harmonization has affected Indian exports and prevented the leveraging of trade agreements adequately.
    - Under the Make in India there is a need to promote ZED manufacturing (Zero effect- Zero Defect) as envisaged.

COVID-19 Pandemic Relief Measures

Collateral-free assistance or sovereign credit guarantees to the Micro, Small and Medium Enterprises (MSMEs) will ease the financial crunch. However, the government should devise this scheme in such a way that the issue of **moral hazard is avoided.**

Weaknesses of the Cgtsme Mode. There are mainly six reasons for banks becoming highly selective in extending credit facilities to MSE borrowers under CGS. The root cause of some of these can be noted in the scheme norms published by CGTMSE itself.

1. The MSME sector is a highly vulnerable sector. The already existing ₹ 29 lakh crore exposure to MSME sector contributes heavily to the non-performing assets (NPAs) of banks. Around 9-10 percent of NPAs of banks are from this segment and it is sufficient reason for banks to reduce exposure to the segment. Even in the loans secured by collaterals, banks find it difficult to recover full amount because of the

deterioration in economic conditions and subsequent erosion in collateral values Higher NPA weakens the balance sheets of banks and banks will have to pump additional capital which is a great challenge in unfavourable economic conditions in the backdrop of the Covid-19 Pandemic.

2. Under the Credit Guarantee Scheme banks have to exercise all due diligence as applicable in the case of other normal lending and have to ascertain project viability. However, strong push by politicians and media coverage create the impression among the public that the government extends guarantee to the banks on liberal terms and that banks are denying the MSE sector what is due to them. Borrowers on this optimistic premise approach banks without homework, proper project and without ascertaining its commercial feasibility or economic viability. The disciplinary actions instituted against bank officials for failed projects deepen the apprehensions of bank officials and increase their reluctance to lend to projects which may or may not take off imperiling their own career prospects.

3. In the case of failed projects, the loss compensated by CGTMSE to the banks is 50/75/80/85 percent of the credit facility. Major part of coverage falls under 75% category and the remaining loss (25% credit facility) has to be absorbed by banks.

   Often PSU banks are under pressure to meet the targets set by the government to make the MSME loan scheme a success, forcing banks to overlook the credit-worthiness of the borrower to meet the heavy targets. Sometimes, bankers face political pressure at local level to give loans to unworthy, politically connected borrowers. This increases the stress in the portfolio and consequent loss to the bank which compels them to deny eligible proposals.

4. Claim under guarantee can be enforced only after satisfying many conditions. Banks can approach CGTMSE for claims only after all required legal actions for recovery are initiated by the bank (except for small loans upto ₹ 50,000 subject to certain conditions). The trust shall pay only 75% of admitted

claims initially. The balance 25% will be paid only on conclusion of recovery proceedings or after initiation of SARFAESI proceedings. This causes the NPA to remain in the balance sheet for long thereby weakening the balance sheet of banks.

5. CGTMSE follows differential risk based pricing for lenders depending upon claim payout. Additional risk premium of 15% will be charged on the applicable rate to lenders who exceed the pay-out threshold limit of 2 times more than the guarantee fee paid, thrice in last 5 years. Higher premium will be applicable for all guaranteed accounts irrespective of the conduct of account. Charging higher fee to well operated accounts becomes a challenge for banks. In addition, higher premium compels genuine borrowers to approach other banks with lower premium. To minimise losses and the premium, banks become very choosy.
6. MSME sector mainly supply their products to major players. However, when the economic conditions go wrong, as it present, in the havoc induced by the COVID-19 Pandemic survival of even big players faces challenges and the demand for the products of MSME sector goes down. Lack of enough capital causes their failure much faster. The failure in turn affects their own future prospects. Under unfavourable circumstances, genuine MSME borrowers explore opportunities to reduce the debt rather than increasing indebtedness despite the presence of guarantee coverage.
7. CGTMSE follows differential risk based pricing for lenders depending upon claim payout. Additional risk premium of 15% will be charged on the applicable rate to lenders who exceed the pay-out threshold limit of 2 times more than the guarantee fee paid, thrice in last 5 years. Higher premium will be applicable for all guaranteed accounts irrespective of the conduct of account. Charging higher fee to well operated accounts becomes a challenge for banks. In addition, higher premium compels genuine borrowers to approach other banks with lower premium. To minimise losses and the premium, banks become very selective.

8. MSME sector mainly supply their products to major players. However, when the economic conditions go wrong, as at present due to the havoc unleashed by the COVID-19 Pandemic survival of even big players faces challenges and the demand for the products of MSME sector goes down. Lack of enough capital causes their failure much faster. The failure in turn affects their own future prospects. Under unfavourable circumstances, genuine MSME borrowers explore opportunities to reduce the debt rather than increasing indebtedness despite the presence of guarantee coverage.

Hence the Banks do not lend despite the guarantee cover and the Atmanirbhar package falters as its pivot is the extension of credit to MSMEs leaning on the crutch of the Credit Guarantee Trust Fund for the MSMEs. Under the credit guarantee scheme for subordinate debt to stressed MSMEs

One time cap of 200 lakh has been removed and CGTSME Guarantee coverage is now on the outstanding exposure per borrower subject to a maximum of 200 crore. Significantly to date only 18 MSMEs (as per CGTSME website www.cgtmse.in have availed the facility. The figure speaks volumes for its perceived efficacy.

Yet the importance of the MSME sector cannot be denied at this stage the sector required relief from GST and also needed working capital loans and support to pay wages to its employees:

1. Employment is a critical need and the manufacturing sector and the new small service units and micro enterprises are the solution. In a labour intensive and capital scarce economy MSEs are the solution to address the problems of unemployment, underemployment and seasonal unemployment all three of which bedevil our economy.
2. Cost of Production: Technological upgradation can serve to reduce the cost of production. Government must help to bring down overheads and fixed costs.
3. Cluster development for the agglomeration effects of development requires much greater attention than it has hitherto recd as Rajeev Joshi in his seminal study on Cluster development in Dhamlka Kutch has pointed out.

4. Marketing support is essential for these industries to scale up.
5. Skill formation and capacity building require attention.
6. Government policy support is essential, this should have a larger component of fiscal incentives.

While China employs 60-80 million workers in manufacturing, India employs 10 to 20 million labour intensive sectors like textiles, garments, leather and footwear, wood and furniture and metal products and petroleum and electrical machinery have great scope for increase of labour intensive production and to increase their share in manufacturing employment.

We have covered some distance but still have a long way to go. Structural reforms and effective oversight and implementation are critical.

Current	***Linked to***	***Investment***
	Manufacturing	Services
Micro	Upto 25 lac	Upto 10 lac
Small	Over 25 lac to 5 crore	Over 10 lac to 2 crore
Medium	Over 5 crore to 10 crore	Over 2 crore to 5 crore

Linked to Turnover

Micro	***Small***	***Medium***
Upto 5 crore	Over 5 crore upto 75 crore	Over 75 crore to 250 crore

Revised classification of MSME			
Classification	micro	small	medium
Manufacturing	investment	investment	investment
Services	Less than 1 crore and turnover less than 5 crore	Less than 10 crore and turnover less than 50 crore	Less than 20 crore and turnover less than 100 crore

In India, MSMEs contribute nearly 8% of the country's GDP, around 45% of the manufacturing output, and approximately 40% of the country's exports. It won't be wrong to refer them as the 'Backbone of the country.'

The Government of India has introduced **MSME or Micro, Small and Medium Enterprises** in agreement with Micro, Small and

Medium Enterprises Development (MSMED) Act of 2006. These enterprises primarily engaged in the production, manufacturing, processing, or preservation of goods and commodities.

MSMEs are an important sector for the Indian economy and have contributed immensely to the country's socio-economic development. It not only generates employment opportunities but also works hand-in-hand towards the development of the nation's backward and rural areas. According to the annual report by the Government (2018-19), there are around 6,08,41,245 MSMEs in India.

MSMEs Redefined

A proposal was made to redefine MSMEs by the Micro, Small and Medium Enterprises Development (Amendment) Bill, 2018, to classify them as manufacturing or service-providing enterprises, based on their annual turnover.

Classification of enterprises into micro, small and medium enterprises (in ₹)

Kind of enterprise	*Act of 2006*		*Bill of 2018*
	Manufacturing	*Services*	*All enterprises*
	Investment towards plant & machinery	*Investment towards equipment*	*Annual Turnover*
Micro	25 lacs	10 lacs	5 Cr
Small	25 lacs to 5 Cr	10 lacs to 2 Cr	5 Cr to 75 Cr
Medium	5 Cr to 10 Cr	2 Cr to 5 Cr	75 Cr to 250

Benefits of the above-proposed reclassification

According to the proposed reclassification or the new classification, there would be no need for frequent inspections to check the investment in plant and machinery. Also, the operations of MSMEs would be transparent, non-discriminatory, and objective in nature.

Highlights of new MSMEs

'Atma Nirbhar Bharat Abhiyan' or the Self-Reliant India Scheme of 2020 by the Government of India has given a new definition for MSMEs.

Following are a few highlighting features of new MSMEs -

Collateral free loans to MSMEs

1. An arrangement of loans to MSMEs, MSME worth of ₹ 3 lac crores.
2. An offer for MSMEs to get a Moratorium period of 12 months.
3. Consideration of Manufacturing and Service MSMEs as the same entities.
4. MSME is a granted a repayment Tenure of 48 months.
5. MSMEs are assured a 100% Credit Guarantee.
6. Reclassification of MSMEs will benefit approximately 45 Lac units.

Features of MSMEs

Following are some of the essential elements of MSMEs -

1. MSMEs work for the welfare of the workers and artisans. They help them by giving employment and by providing loans and other services.
2. MSMEs provide credit limit or funding support to banks.
3. They promote the development of entrepreneurship as well as up-gradation of skills by launching specialized training centers for the same.
4. They support the up-grading of developmental technology, infrastructure development, and the modernization of the sector as a whole.
5. MSMEs are known to provide reasonable assistance for improved access to the domestic as well as export markets.
6. They also offer modern testing facilities and quality certification services.
7. Following the recent trends, MSMEs now support product development, design innovation, intervention, and packaging.

Role of MSMEs in Indian Economy

Since its formation, the MSME segment has proven to be a highly dynamic Indian economy sector. MSMEs produce and manufacture a variety of products for both domestic as well as international markets. They have helped promote the growth and development of khadi, village, and coir industries. They have collaborated and worked with the concerned ministries, state governments, and stakeholders towards the upbringing of rural areas.

MSMEs have played an essential role in providing employment opportunities in rural areas. They have helped in the industrialization of these areas with a low capital cost compared to the large industries. Acting as a complementary unit to large sectors, the MSME sector has enormously contributed to its socio-economic development.

MSMEs also contribute and play an essential role in the country's development in different areas like the requirement of low investment, flexibility in operations, mobility through the locations, low rate of imports, and a high contribution to domestic production.

With the capability and capacity to develop appropriate local technology, provide fierce competition in domestic and international markets, technology-savvy industries, a contribution towards creating defence materials, and generating new entrepreneurs by providing knowledge, training, and skill up-gradation through specialized training centers.

The below-mentioned data, represented in a tabular format, is by the Central Statistics Office (CSO) and Ministry of Statistics & Programme Implementation.

Contribution of MSMEs in Country's Economy at Current Price

Year	*MSME-Addition of Gross Value*	*Growth (%)*	*Total Addition of Gross Value*	*Share of MSME in GVA (%)*	*Total GDP*	*Share of MSME in GDP (in %)*
2011-12	2622574	–	8106946	32.35	8736329	30
2012-13	3020528	15.17	9202692	32.82	9944013	30.40
2013-14	3389922	12.23	10363153	32.71	11233522	30.20
2014-15	3704956	9.29	11504279	32.21	12467959	29.70
2015-16	4025595	8.65	12566646	32.03	13764037	29.20
2016-17	4405753	9.44	13841591	31.83	15253714	28.90

Source: Central Statistics Office (CSO), Ministry of Statistics & Programme Implementation.

Importance of MSMEs for the Indian Economy

Across the globe, MSMEs are accepted as a means of economic growth and for promoting equitable development. They are known to generate the highest rate of growth in the economy. MSMEs have driven India to new heights through requirements of low investment, flexible operations, and the capacity to develop appropriate technology.

1. MSMEs employ around 120 million persons, becoming the second-largest employment generating sector after agriculture.
2. With approximately 45 lac units throughout the country, it contributes about 6.11% of GDP from manufacturing and 24.63% of the GDP from service activities.
3. MSME ministry targets to increase its contribution towards GDP by up to 50% by 2025 as India moves ahead to become a $5 trillion economy.
4. Contributing around 45% of overall Indian exports.
5. MSMEs promote all-inclusive growth by providing employment opportunities, especially to people belonging to weaker sections of the society in rural areas.
6. MSMEs in tier-2 and tier-3 cities help in creating opportunities for people to use banking services and products, which can amount to the final inclusion of the contribution of MSMEs for the economy.
7. MSMEs promote innovation by providing an opportunity to budding entrepreneurs to help them build creative products they and thereby boost competition in business and fuel the growth.

Challenges to MSME

- Absence of adequate and timely banking finance.
- Limited capital and knowledge.
- Non-availability of suitable technology.
- Low production capacity.
- Ineffective marketing strategy.

- Constraints on modernisation and expansions.
- Non-availability of skilled labour at affordable cost.

Persistent and Perceived Barriers to Growth

I. Despite the MSME sector contributing significantly to the economy, it continues to face several challenges. The major challenges include physical infrastructure bottlenecks; absence of formalisation; inertia to technology adoption; capacity building; backward and forward linkages; lack of access to credit and risk capital; and the perennial problem of delayed payments, among others.

II. Infrastructure bottlenecks and Competition

- Notwithstanding various efforts to upgrade the infrastructure, the MSME clusters, particularly the micro enterprises, are inadequately equipped with necessary support systems which not only impede their day-to-day business operations but also their future growth prospects. While infrastructure constraint is only one side of the story, MSMEs also need to do their bit to improve competitiveness. They need to shed their inhibition to adopt new technologies; accept e-payments; and foster in-house innovation which will help them manage their businesses digitally and compete globally. Given the current scenario of global trade, the age-old methods of operating business with low levels of technology adoption deprives them of potential economies of scale. Lack of expertise in product development, designing, packaging and marketing strategy due to their small size add up to the pressure of adapting to the changing environment around them. The strategy for MSMEs should be to gradually expand in size and reduce the dependence on the incentive structure provided by the government. Their aim should be eventually to compete on a global scale.

III. Lack of Access to Credit and Formalisation

- Credit plays a vital role in development of MSME sector

as funds at a reasonable cost can increase their competitiveness. Credit disbursal to this sector has, however, remained sluggish in recent periods. At an aggregate level, the total credit outstanding from banks and NBFCs to the MSME sector was approximately 16.6 lakh crore as at end of September, 2019. Scheduled commercial banks account for 90 percent of the share of total credit outstanding.

IV. As many MSMEs mainly operate in the informal space, assessing their credit-worthiness can be difficult due to information asymmetry, particularly with respect to the financial performance of their businesses. In the absence of collateral, under-writing the customer often entails higher operating cost. Furthermore, due to their small-scale operations, MSMEs are not able to raise risk capital.

V. They are also unable to take advantage of most of the government schemes which are mostly based on digital infrastructure and require beneficiaries to have some form of digital identity and presence. Despite the implementation of structural reforms like GST and JAM trinity, the informal units are, however, not getting integrated with the mainstream in recent years.

VI. Delayed Payments

A large number of MSMEs are ancillary units catering to the needs of large industries, both in the public and private sector. They often face the problem of delayed payments, affecting their cash flow and working capital availability. Most of the time, delay in realisation of such receivables increases their operating cycle and reduces their ability to procure new orders or fulfil the existing ones. A primary survey conducted by Reserve Bank in December 2019 showed that 44 percent of MSMEs engaged in manufacturing activities faced delay in payments. The ones not receiving timely payment mainly belonged to basic metal and metal products, engineering, construction and infrastructure related industries. On the other hand, delay in payments was lower at 27 percent for services sector. Here transport operators mostly faced such situations. Although Micro, Small and Medium Enterprises Development (MSMED) Act, 2006 contains provisions related to penalty in case of delayed payments by the buyers, weak bargaining power and the fear of losing the business prevents MSMEs to invoke this provision.

VII. PROBLEMS DUE TO THE REVISED DEFINITION OF THE INSOLVENCY AND BANKRUPTCY CODE: Recent changes in the Insolvency and Bankruptcy Code (IBC), raising the threshold for invoking insolvency to ₹ 1 crore from ₹ 1 lakh, is among one of the reasons MSMEs are finding it difficult to recover their dues from large corporates. Even as government departments have started clearing up dues of MSMEs with the Finance Ministry stressing timely clearance of funds, many micro and small firms are stuck with pending payments of more than ₹ 3 lakh crore with large firms with no easy legal recourse.

Industry sources said the IBC had empowered many small companies with dues of — say ₹ 40-50 lakh — to get their dues cleared by threatening to take bigger companies to NCLT for non-payment. This gave them a negotiating lever in early clearance of their dues, because a company being dragged to National Company Law Tribunal can have adverse ramifications. On March 24, the government decided to raise "the threshold of default under Section 4 of the IBC 2016 to ₹ 1 crore" due to emerging financial distress for most companies. While the intention was to provide some breathing space to companies facing distress due to pandemic, it had an unintended effect of slowing down payments by big corporates to smaller firms.

"Even a small company doing a monthly billing of ₹ 1 crore usually has pending payments of ₹ 30-40 lakhs. Now they are stuck. They can request for clearance of dues, stop partial supplies but cannot use the IBC," said KE Raghunathan, convener of the Consortium of MSME associations. The threshold for invoking insolvency could have been raised 10 times to ₹ 10 lakh instead of it being raised 100 times to ₹ 1 crore, as that would prevent most frivolous cases being filed under the law, he said. MSMEs used this legal provision as a bargaining tool to get their dues on time and it worked in many cases.

Recent changes in the Insolvency and Bankruptcy Code (IBC), raising the threshold for invoking insolvency to ₹ 1 crore from ₹ 1 lakh, is among one of the reasons MSMEs are finding it difficult to recover their dues from large corporates. Even as government departments have started clearing up dues of MSMEs with the Finance Ministry stressing timely clearance of funds, many micro and small firms are stuck with pending payments of more than ₹ 3 lakh crore with large firms with no easy legal recourse.

As per a recent Brickwork Ratings study, MSMEs have nearly ₹ 3.3 lakh crore of their funds stuck with strong large corporates in form of receivables. "The liquidity crunch being faced by MSMEs is on account of two key issues, including the lack of a funding line from the banking system and stretched working capital because of low bargaining power with large corporates to have payments released," it said.

VIII. PANDEMIC PROBLEMS: The pandemic has led to large corporates being on a much stronger footing financially compared to smaller firms especially since April who have lost bargaining power to claim dues. Reduction in days for which dues are pending would substantially improve liquidity conditions for MSMEs. While banks have started disbursing funds to MSMEs under the 100 percent Emergency Credit Line Guarantee Scheme announced by government last month, credit availability remains a challenge for stressed firms.

IX. THE INSOLVENCY AND BANKRUPTCY CODE AND ITS DISCONTENTS: Till March, 2020, 157 corporate insolvency resolution plans were withdrawn under Section 12A of the IBC, of which 64 cases involved amounts less than ₹ 1 crore, as per data from the Insolvency and Bankruptcy Board of India. The reasons for early withdrawal of cases were full settlement with the applicant and other settlement with creditors.

"The IBC law is working as a deterrent as many times debtors settle the case on receipt of a notice for repayment. In many cases, we have observed that dues are recovered after an application is filed but before it's admitted by the NCLT bench. Settlement prior to admission of the case cost effective for both parties and it works well for smaller companies," said a Delhi-based lawyer. Even for banks and financial institutions, IBC has resulted in higher recoveries compared to other platforms.

As a percentage of claims, banks recovered on average 42.5 percent of the amount filed through the IBC in 2018-19, against 14.5 percent through the SARFAESI, 5.3 percent through Lok Adalats and 3.5 percent through Debt Recovery Tribunals, as per latest available RBI data.

Expert Committee on MSMEs

Adding to the plethora of Committees whose recommendations languish and are seldom acted upon and followed up. In order to understand the structural bottlenecks and factors affecting the performance of the MSMEs, RBI had set up an Expert Committee on MSMEs under the Chairmanship of Shri U.K. Sinha in January 2019. The Committee has undertaken comprehensive review of the sector and given several recommendations for the economic and financial sustainability of the MSME sector. These recommendations are wide ranging and broadly relate to legislative changes; infrastructure development; capacity building; technological upgradation; improving backward and forward linkages; improving financial support from formal sources; newer technological interventions for robust underwriting practices; and credit delivery, among others. While some of the recommendations of the Committee have already been implemented, others are under consideration by the authorities concerned.

RBI Measures to Improve the Credit Flow

ENABLING BANKS TO LEND THROUGH NBFCs: The Reserve Bank has taken several measures in the recent period to improve the flow of credit to the MSME sector. Banks form the predominant source of formal credit to MSMEs with all such loans by banks qualifying for Priority Sector Lending classification. In August 2019 RBI enabled banks to lend to MSMEs through the NBFC sector. Consequently, bank credit to registered NBFCs (other than Micro Finance Institutions) for on-lending to micro and small enterprises up to 20 lakh per borrower are eligible for classification as priority sector lending.

One Time Restructuring

A scheme of one-time restructuring without an asset classification downgrade was permitted to GST registered MSME accounts that were in default but standard as on January 1, 2019. As the process of formalisation of the MSME sector has a positive impact on financial stability and this process is still underway, the scheme has been extended to accounts that are standard but in default as on January 1, 2020 and restructuring, wherever eligible, has to be implemented latest by December 31, 2020. This will enhance the scope of the scheme by benefitting the eligible MSME entities which could not be restructured under the provisions of the circular dated January 1, 2019 as also the MSME entities which have become stressed thereafter. So far, banks have restructured 6 lakh accounts out of 15 lakh eligible accounts under the scheme. RBI primary survey suggested lack of awareness about the scheme among the MSME.

CRR Exemptions on Incremental Loans to Incentivise Banks to Lend to MSME Sector

Incremental loans to MSMEs along with retail loans for automobiles and residential housing will be exempted from CRR from fortnight ending January 31, 2020 up to fortnight ending July 31, 2020.

External Benchmark for MSME Loans

Subsequent to the introduction of an external benchmark system in October 2019, the monetary policy transmission has improved where new floating rate loans to the micro and small entrepreneurs were linked to the external benchmark. With a view to further strengthening monetary policy transmission, all new floating rate loans to medium enterprises extended by banks from April 01, 2020 will also be linked to the external benchmarks.

Resolving Delay in Receipt of Payments

Delay in getting payments is one of the perennial problems faced by MSMEs. To address this issue, the Reserve Bank introduced the Trade Receivables Discounting System (TReDS) in 2014. TReDS is an electronic platform where receivables of MSMEs drawn against buyers (large corporates, PSUs, Government departments) are financed through multiple financiers at competitive rates. This is done through an auction-based mechanism. To widen the scope of TReDS and to incentivise more players to be part of this platform, banks' exposure through this platform were brought under priority sector lending in 2016.

Entities Under TReDS

Presently, three entities [viz., Receivables Exchange of India Ltd. (RXIL), A. TReDS, and Mynd Solutions] licensed by the Reserve Bank are operating the platform for more than two years. Further, the Reserve Bank recently allowed 'on tap' authorization to entities desirous to provide platforms for TReDS. Hence, in coming years, competition in receivables discounting space is bound to increase with the entry of new players. This requires the corporates, both in the public and private sector, to join the TReDS platform and make the system more efficient.

Mandatory Registration TReDS

In 2018, the Government made it mandatory for all companies with a turnover greater than ₹ 500 crores to register with TReDS. As on February 2020, while 8211 MSME sellers were registered while only

1530 buyers were participating on the platforms. Trade Bodies should encourage and handhold all its members to participate in the TReDS platform.

Union Budget App Based Invoice Financing

In the Union Budget 2020-21, the Government has announced app-based invoice financing products to obviate the problem of delayed payments of MSME. The mechanism may prove complementary to the TReDS platform and would further alleviate the problem of delayed payments.

Policy Choices and the Way Forward

The MSME sector holds immense potential, the need is to have a right set of policies and enabling framework which guide and support MSMEs to effectively handle their existing problems and venture into new areas. While both the Government and the RBI have introduced a plethora of measures for improving access to finance and to promote growth of the sector, the small size of individual units and informal nature of the sector continue to pose challenges. The biggest challenge lies not in the formulation of policies but in their implementation.

Fin Tech and its Usage for MSME Loan Appraisal

The traditional bank lending system by banks is based on financial statements and collateral of the borrower. With increased availability of data from several sources, including GSTN, income tax, credit bureaus, etc., it is now possible to appraise the MSME loan proposals expeditiously by doing due diligence online. Further, with the help of Account Aggregators (AA), lenders will have access to potential borrower's financial information at a single point, of course, with his/ her consent. Furthermore, emergence of FinTech companies has made it possible to assess credit worthiness of MSMEs by utilising unexplored data sources such as digital transaction trails, data generated through e-commerce sites, etc. Some lenders are collaborating with FinTech companies to take advantage of such surrogate data for speedier credit underwriting for extending loans to MSME sector. These new architectures would expand the reach of credit.

TRADITIONAL LENDING AND CREDIT APPRAISAL: While the new models are beneficial for those units which are digitally active, a large segment of MSME units access credit through traditional lending models. While micro enterprises act as a starting stage of entrepreneurship that requires low investment in technology, units graduating to small and medium enterprises have to enhance their technical capacity and explore newer markets in order to stay competitive for sustainable growth. Recent policy efforts will provide an enabling environment and facilitate the MSME sector seize the new emerging opportunities. RBI to safeguard financial stability while ensuring wider access to finance. Banks and other players on their part have to ensure prudent lending.

Innovation Regulatory Sandbox RBI Cohorts

RBI have started launching cohorts under the Regulatory Sandbox. First such cohort was launched in November 2019 with the theme of 'Retail Payments' to spur innovation in digital payments space to design and test newer payment services for the unserved and underserved segments. In due course, it proposes to run a regulatory sandbox for cohorts focussed on lending. This would promote innovation in MSME lending segment.

Public Credit Registry

The project on Public Credit Registry (PCR) will fundamentally address the information asymmetry that impedes access to credit for micro and small entrepreneurs. The PCR has been envisaged as a database of core credit information. The registry would play crucial role in reducing credit gap in the segment.

Integration with Global Value Chains

Given the fact that the MSME sector contributes significantly to exports, it is essential that they should be integrated with Global Value Chains (GVC) to remain competitive as it offers unique opportunity to become technologically and digitally empowered. Being part of GVC would enable MSMEs to produce quality goods and services which will have greater acceptability in the global market. The major challenges for the sector to connect to the GVC are lack of information, knowledge of markets and quality standards.

The World Bank's Board of Executive Directors has approved a $750 million MSME Emergency Response programme to support funding to micro, small and medium enterprises (MSMEs), severely impacted by the COVID-19 pandemic.

The programme will help in improving funding capacity of Small Finance Banks (SFBs) and Non-Banking Financial Companies (NBFCs) for the MSME sector.

The World Bank said this programme will address the immediate liquidity and credit needs of some 1.5 million viable MSMEs to help them withstand the impact of the current shock and protect millions of jobs. The loan has a maturity of 19 years including a five-year grace period.

International technology markets are imperfect, and finding the right technology in The Report of the Working Group on Micro, Small and Medium Enterprises (MSMEs) growth for 12th Five Year Plan (2012-17), unveils that the sector accounts for 45% of the manufacturing output and 40% of the total exports of the country. Further the Ministry of MSME's (2017), highlights that the MSMEs accounted for 30.74% of GDP in the year 2014-15. Current economic forecast or survey interprets that with the Indian Economy growing at an average of 7% per annum, it is likely to become a $5 trillion economy by the year 2025. Hence, the development of the MSME sector becomes essential as it is considered to be the backbone of India.

However, in spite of high growth rate and good prospects, the Indian MSMEs have been subject to certain constraints. The most notable barriers are lack of timely credit, Procurement of raw materials at competitive cost, inadequate infrastructure facilities including power, water, road, and lack of skilled manpower for manufacturing, services, marketing, etc. The most important constraints faced till date are technological backwardness.

The Indian MSMEs lack up-to-date information and are often unaware about the latest technologies present in the global market.

Sometimes they lack managerial skills, entrepreneurial knowledge and technology-intensive education to run a competent MSME. This type of problem normally prevails in the rural-based areas. It is said that Information Communication and Technology (ICT) can play a bigger role for MSMEs as they face stiffer competition from their rival neighbouring countries (China, Indonesia, Philippines and Thailand). Hence, the need of the hour is upgradation of technology. For Indian MSME's to become competitive, it has to adopt the best international practices and constantly upgrade its technology. It is often found that the main challenge for many Small and Medium Enterprises (SMEs) is to cultivate right skills and management practices for establishing and integrating knowledge created by external partners with in-house practices and innovation processes (OECD).

Technology Upgradation and its Constraints

1. The SMEs engaged in developing countries normally produce traditional items (inferior quality) accompanied with low productivity. They mainly cater to the small local markets. Hence, an accelerated technical change within a short span of time making the SMEs difficult to establish a competitive advantage in the global market.
2. Adoption of new skills in the right manner is quite a cumbersome task. Also mastering of a new technology involves acquiring new skills, materials and methods which can uncertain and a costly process. *Adopting and innovating technology are critical to the success of SMEs in the process of internationalization.* SMEs needs to be use the latest technologies to generate efficient and high-quality production, and compete in the global market. The new concepts such as cloud computing, which enable cooperative sharing of resources, will help smaller firms to leverage on the advanced technologies. Such arrangements free up critical resources of MSMEs, and lead to more focusing on the core activities.
3. *Lack of access and investment in technology hinders the ability of MSMEs to compete in global markets.* Technology is a key differentiator for the MSME sector to remain globally

competitive. With the ongoing global trend, Indian MSMEs has their own set of challenges related to technology adoption and scale of operations.

The other compelling reasons behind adoption of new/advanced technology are requirement to adhere to regulatory norms related to (i) effluent discharge norms, (ii) product quality certifications (domestic/exports) etc. may be a pre-requisite for MSMEs to continue supplying to global markets with strict regulatory rules, policy support and numerous schemes implemented by government bodies in aiding technology upgradation, necessity for upgradation of technology and withdrawal of maintenance support for existing technology may force MSMEs to adopt new technology, and lastly, lack of availability of requisite level of skills among the labour force even for normal jobs a prominent reason behind MSMEs for rapid technology adoption.

However, MSMEs may fail to take the complete advantages of globalization if some additional barriers exist such as lack of digital access, insufficient resources or knowledge to innovate the product quality, inability to lower the export prices, higher unit cost of production, informational bottlenecks, inadequate strategy for marketing and advertising.

India needs to put in place comprehensive policy frameworks to boost long term economic growth. To move into the global supply chains swiftly to replace the Chinese dragon we need to address the Export issue effectively so that we continue to accrue foreign exchange gains bolstering our foreign exchange reserves, our balance sheet, and our ability to service our external debt. The traditional goods exported from India were Textiles and readymade garments. Despite the advantages of cheap labour supply chains have relocated to Thailand, Bangladesh and Vietnam. For cheap manufacture of these products we have to move quickly to fill this niche so that we become an outsourcing destination for production of readymade garments. The Economic survey has proposed. "Assemble in India for the world" into "Make in India" to achieve an unprecedented opportunity to chart a China-like, labour-intensive, export trajectory that was witnessed till recent times.

Traditional Exports from India where there is tremendous untapped potential comprise:

1. Regional Handicrafts - Native Art and Artefacts
2. Organic Supplements and Herbs
3. Medicines and Spices as Turmeric for alternative healing
4. Meat and Sea Food Exports through extensive aquaculture
5. Dairy and dairy supplements (Amul exports to China, Japan, Myanmar, Afghanistan, Africa, Malaysia and a host of other countries.)
6. Gems, Jewellery, Precious Stones
7. Leather and Leather Products
8. Ceramics
9. Petroleum Products (Charcoal, coal, Pet coke).

Trade liberalisation can effectively promote development by allowing the optimal allocation of resources in an economy

Ease of doing business demands greater attention.

Look for Greenfield products and unexplored markets.

Create new infrastructure upgrade and modernize existing infrastructure

Ensure a technological facelift to the sector.

A SWOT analysis of the Export landscape throws up the following interesting vignettes:

Strengths

Business strengths are its resources and capabilities that can be used as a basis for developing a competitive-advantage. Examples of such strengths include:

- Patents.
- Strong brand names.
- Good reputation among customers.
- Cost advantages from proprietary know-how.
- Exclusive access to high grade natural resources.
- Favourable access to distribution networks.

Weaknesses

The absence of certain strengths may be viewed as a weakness. For example, each of the following may be considered weaknesses:

- Lack of patent protection.
- A weak brand name.
- Poor reputation among customers.
- High cost structure.
- Lack of access to the best natural resources.
- Lack of access to key distribution channels.

Opportunities

The external environmental analysis may reveal certain new opportunities for profit and growth. Some examples of such opportunities include:

- An unfulfilled customer need.
- Arrival of new technologies.
- Loosening of regulations.
- Removal of international trade barriers.

Threats comprise the obverse, the increase in protectionist barriers

- High Tariffs
- Prohibitive Cost Structures

Targeting the Right Market is important

1. Geographical Factors
    - Country, state, region,
    - Time zones,
    - Urban/rural location,
    - Logistical considerations e.g. freight and distribution channels.
2. Economic, Political, and Legal Environmental Factors
    - Regulations including quarantine,
    - Labelling standards,

- Standards and consumer protection rules,
- Duties and taxes.

3. Demographic Factors
    - Age and gender,
    - Income and family structure,
    - Occupation,
    - Cultural beliefs,
    - Major competitors,
    - Similar products,
    - Key brands.
4. Market Characteristics
    - Market size,
    - Availability of domestic manufacturers,
    - Agents, distributors and suppliers.

Changes in the external environmental also may present threats to the firm. Some examples of such threats include:

- Shifts in consumer tastes away from the firm's products.
- Emergence of substitute products.
- New regulations.
- Increased trade barriers.
- The product should be manufactured or sourced with consistent standard quality, comparable to competitor countries.
- ISO or equivalent certification helps in selling the product in the international market.
- Avoid products which are monopoly of one or few suppliers. For manufacturering - make sure sufficient capacity is available in-house or the wherewithal to outsource it at short notice. Timely supply is a key success factor in export business.
- The price of the exported product should not fluctuate very often - threatening profitability to the export business.
- Strictly check the government policies related to the export of a particular product. Though there are very few restrictions

in export - it is better to check regulatory status of your selected product.

- Carefully study the various government incentive schemes and tax exemption like duty drawback and DEPB.
- Import regulation in overseas markets, specially tariff and non-tariff barriers. Though a major non-tariff barrier (textile quota) has been abolished - there are still other tariff and non-tariff barriers. If your product attracts higher duty in target country - demand obviously falls.
- Registration/Special provision for your products in importing country. This is specially applicable for processed food and beverages, drugs and chemicals. WTO norms have to be met.
- Seasonal vagaries of selected products as some products sell in summer, while others in winter. Festive season is also important factor, for example certain products are more sellable only during Christmas.
- Keep in mind special packaging and labeling requirements of perishable products like processed food and dairy products.
- Special measures are required for transportation of certain products, which may be bulky or fragile or hazardous or perishable.

Build Faster, Bigger and Better Value Chains

Technological developments have opened up a variety of possibilities for the Export sector.

Internet of Things (IOT) and data analysis have to be harnessed for increasing, our productivity, and production marketing and the necessary benchmarking to International Standards.

It is clear that China, which undoubtedly has been the biggest beneficiary of this process of globalization, will be under pressure. The one time global factory of the world was already under pressure as global trade started to shrink, a trade war with the US escalated and its own internal fiscal excesses have begun to catch up; the devastation caused by Covid-19, which incidentally originated in Wuhan, will make it extremely difficult. For Indian Exports capacity augmentation can open up new opportunities. The US-led battle with China puts pressure on global majors to diversify their supply chains. To benefit from Global Supply Chains, India's exports must command higher value by making the leap of faith, up the value chain instead of being restricted to manufacturing activities. We need to scale up and fast by building capacities of local manufacturers both in terms of skill and scale. These domestic entities should be able to forge mutually beneficial relationships with foreign technology partners in terms of skill. These domestic entities should be able to forge mutually beneficial relationships with foreign technology partners. China deleveraging presents an opportunity for India to move into the vacuum. It also presents an opportunity for India to pitch itself as a viable, high end alternative to China in the Global Supply Chain (GSC) with as the Prime Minister has often iterated skill, scale and speed.

Imports from China Urgent need for Import Substitution

India's largest import from China are mobile phone components worth 7.2 billion in 2018-19 comprising 9% of total imports these form the foundation of a "Make in India" policy for mobile phones which is essentially assemble in India.

Second, third, and fourth imports are computers and components, electrical circuits and components, and semi-conductor chips that compounded together constitute an additional chunk of imports.

Globalisation

Globalization normally results in free movement of goods and services across the borders. High tariff walls (i.e. Import tax, quotas or voluntary export restraints) imposed by the importing nations, may prevent the MSMEs to compete in the global market. Again, there may be situations where MSMEs producing textile goods face a tough competition with their rivals producing synthetic products. The rival may capture a higher market share with the use of higher level of technology and skilled man-power. The Indian MSME may fail to compete in such situations. The private sector has not been the recipient of growth to the expected levels. The Atma Nirbhar package strives to redress this by recognizing that large segments of the

Economy, such as small and medium enterprises and rural households remain excluded from formal finance. There is a wide ranging consensus, especially in the face of the Pandemic on what needs to be done the real challenge lies in doing it.

This involves putting in place detailed design and implementation of these reforms.

The private sector has not been the recipient of growth to the expected levels. The Atma Nirbhar package strives to redress this by recognizing that large segments of the Economy, such as small and medium enterprises and rural households remain excluded from formal finance. There is a wide ranging consensus, especially in the face of the Pandemic on what needs to be done the real challenge lies in doing it.

This involves putting in place detailed design and implementation of these reforms.

In the post-covid world as we have pointed out in Chapter 1 the major characteristic will be Economic Nationalism this will further scupper the field for the MSME sector.

Chapter - V

The Indian - Banks

The Lynch pin of the entire economic recovery effort are the banks, the development of the financial system is critical to sustain economic growth necessary for taking India to a high growth trajectory, the designated partners in progress are the Public Sector Banks. Banks financial institutions are burdened heavily with non-performing loans and frauds. Government has not budgeted any capital inflows for fresh PSBs recapitalisation. Basel regulations are set to sleep for quite some time with Europe and West fighting to survive the pandemic risk shocks. Balance sheet size by itself is not going to be the point of confidence so much as delivery on credit for the promised sectorial reforms for leading the economic rebound. The backdrop of slowing domestic economic activity lends no comfort. There is increasing uncertainty of heightened spillovers from global markets and global economic seizures.

Widening Access, Maintaining Financial Stability

The Financial Sector continues to be straddled by the Public Sector Banks. In an increasingly liberalized environment sharp challenges confront our Policy-makers and our Banks. The endeavour is to create a efficient financial system that increases and widens access while maintaining financial stability. Are the banks in a position to measure up? will they be able to deliver on the promises made by government through the Atma Nirbhar Package for which Banks are the delivery mechanisms.

The reforms which have been undertaken in the financial sector in the decades from 1991 have undoubtedly improved the soundness and depth of the financial sector and led to an impressive growth in the country's financial resources however much more is required to be done to ensure the efficient allocation of these resources to finance the higher levels of investment necessary for sustained growth and poverty reduction in the paradigm of the post covid era.

Strategic Sector

As part of the Atmanirbhar Package the centre proposes to designate the banking/financial sector as a strategic sector. We need to enhance the viability and overall efficiency of our banking system. Under the new Atmanirbhar Bharat dispensation the government intends to designate some sectors as strategic sectors and in each sector no more than four state-owned companies will exist, this means that the Banks which have not faced mergers so far IOB, PSB, UCO and Bank of Maharashtra may be merged or privatised.

Banking Sector Recent Reforms and Emerging Challenges

India's Financial Sector is characterized by a dominance of Public Sector Banks; they score on large branch networks, brand image and Public confidence that they are too big to fail. They would be bailed out, recapitalized by the government therefore they are "Safe". These assumptions are partially correct, however, this does not detract from the fact that the operating environment is getting tougher, and that there is a tradeoff between efficiency and improved financial and operational performance, the one is no longer a corollary of the other.

The Indian Financial System is dominated by Banks. Within Banks, the Public Sector Banks hold sway, the Financial institutions include the development Finance Institutions like NABARD and SIDBI, Insurance companies, and Housing Finance Companies the Non Bank Finance Companies include the asset finance companies and microfinance companies, the Mutual Funds include Large Cap, Mid Cap, Small Cap, and Provident and Pension Funds. Strong banks, weak Banks, large Banks, small banks, rural and urban, public and private, new and old private sector banks, cooperative banks, primary agriculture societies, foreign banks which are largely corporate Banks lending to large corporate, small finance banks, local area banks, payment banks coexist. The distribution of Banks as per profitability indices is skewed. Private Banks come with the latest technology and younger better trained personnel in place, who can also be brash in lending decisions and like the wunderkind Nick Leeson, bet the bank. While gargantuan Public Sector Banks struggle to maintain Capital Adequacy and have stodgy, conservative rule bound personnel who will not move a centimeter away from the rule book. Changes have been ushered in, the entry of new players has increased competition, a few banks earn high returns and operate efficiently, others compete fiercely for the same tiny market segment.

Advantages of Consolidation

Consolidation improves the structure and efficiency of the banking system. Well executed mergers reduce the cost of operations, expand the business profile, enhance growth, and increase the capital base and the risk taking ability. The Narasimhan Committee had suggested the Brahmanical structure of three or four large Banks, with International presence, eight to ten domestic banks with a National presence, Local Banks with a regional presence and rural banks. The committee suggested merger among strong banks and weak banks with financial institutions and Non Bank Finance companies. The mergers which took place in the early 1990s were that of the New Bank of India with the Punjab National Bank. In 1998, 20th Century Finance merged with Centurion Bank. In 1999, Bareilly Corporation Bank merged with Bank of Baroda and Sikkim Bank with Union Bank of India. In February 2000, Times Bank merged with HDFC Bank and in March 2001, Bank of Madura merged with ICICI bank. ICICI Ltd ad a reverse merger with the ICICI bank in 31st March 2000 the Benares State Bank Ltd merged with Bank of Baroda on June 29, 2000, Global Trust Bank merged with the Oriental Bank of Commerce from August 14, 2004, as per a scheme approved under the Banking Regulation Act and sanctioned by the Government. PNB took over New Bank of India in 1993 and acquired Nedungadi Bank in 2005, 2005-6 saw the amalgamation of the Ganesh Bank of

Kurundwad with the Federal Bank Ltd as its net worth turned negative and there was a voluntary amalgamation between Bank of Punjab Ltd and the Centurion Bank Ltd. The Centurion Bank subsequently changed its name to Centurion Bank of Punjab Ltd and merged with HDFC Bank on May 23rd 2008, The United Western Bank was placed under Moratorium and amalgamated with the Industrial Development Bank Ltd in 2006. The Sangli Bank and the Bank of Rajasthan were merged with the ICICI Bank. Consolidation is required.

1. Exploit Synergies
2. Cost Cutting
3. Increased Capital Base
4. Acquire New Markets
5. Increase risk ability.

Internatinal Rules and Regulations for Banks Globally

With implementation of the initiatives taken by the

1. International bodies, policy makers across jurisdictions have been strengthening regulatory frameworks.
2. Due to the stringency of the Basel norms the capital position of banks has improved consistently in major advanced and emerging market economies as a result of various regulatory reforms introduced after the global financial crisis. These policies may help in the medium to long run by enhancing the soundness and resilience of the global banking system.
3. The Pandemic has had a disastrous effect on credit growth, which has decelerated across major economies. This, in turn, has adversely affected bank profitability.
4. Despite distinct improvement in asset quality, structural weaknesses like continued overreliance on investment in government securities in the Euro area and wholesale funding in many advanced economies remain problematic for global banks.

II. Indian Scenario

SBI is the only Bank large enough to meet the cut of being a global Bank.

Reserve Bank of India, has ensured that Banks are compliant with Basel standards and largely adhering to them in terms of countercyclical capital buffer (CCCB); capital requirements for central counter-parties (CCPs); leverage ratio framework; Liquidity Coverage Ratio (LCR); Net Stable Funding Ratio (NSFR); Domestic-Systemically Important Banks (D-SIBs) requirements; and a Supervisory framework for measuring and controlling large exposures.

Resolutions through the Insolvency and Bankruptcy Code (IBC)

Resolution frameworks do not inspire much confidence the IBC was more totemic than real as the resolution process continued to be tardy under the IBC and now it has been placed in suspended animation for the next six months due to the Covid Pandemic this does not lend much comfort, and does not augur well.

Impact of Covid-19 Post August 2020 on the Asset Quality of the Banks

The Banking sector despite recapitalization and improvement in asset quality invites serious concern. Capital position of banks has, however, improved on account of recapitalization of public sector banks by the government and capital raising efforts by private sector banks. Profitability of the banking sector remains fragile. The moratorium has been extended by RBI till August post August there is expected to be recognition and consequently rise in impaired assets and a significant increase in provisioning. Nevertheless, the sector continues to encounter challenges from events like those around the telecom sector, automobile, housing, real estate aviation sector, the slowing of the economy and the overall deleterious impact of the Pandemic. The impact of COVID-19 and the associated policy response is likely to result in an additional ₹ 1,67,000 crore of debt from the top 500 debt-heavy private sector borrowers turning delinquent between FY21 and FY22, a rating agency said. In the worst-case scenario, corporate stress could increase further by ₹ 1.68 lakh crore.

"This is over and above the ₹ 2,54,000 crore anticipated prior to the onset of pandemic, taking the cumulative quantum to ₹ 421,000 crore," India Ratings and Research (Ind-Ra) said in a report. This constitutes 6.63 percent of the total debt (previous estimate: 4 per cent). Given that 11.57 percent of the outstanding debt is already stressed, the proportion of stressed debt is likely to increase to 18.21 percent of the outstanding quantum. The corresponding credit cost is expected to be 3.57 percent of the total debt, Ind-Ra said.

The agency said in a scenario wherein funding markets continue to exhibit heightened risk aversion, corporate stress could increase further by ₹ 1.68 lakh crore, resulting in ₹ 5.89 lakh crore of the corporate debt (9.27 percent of the total debt) becoming stressed in FY21-FY22. The resultant credit cost could be higher at 4.82 percent of the outstanding book. Consequently, 20.84 percent of the outstanding debt could be under stress in the agency's stress case scenario, it said.

Non-Performing Assets

Consequently, the overhang of non-performing assets (NPAs) is expected to increase. This will further constrain the banks ability to meet the credit needs and will impair economic revival. Before the pandemic low profitability and deleveraging by certain corporates, had led risk-averse banks to shift from the loan book to the retail book. In a slowing economy this had the nasty effect of increasing the pool of bad assets. Further, sector-wise the distressed sectors hit by the Pandemic need policy attention. Though the Banking sector has primarily to channelise credit to MSMEs and other identified segments under the Atma Nirbhar Programme, proper due diligence and risk pricing in lending is of prime importance so that the health of the banking sector is not compromised while ensuring adequate flow of credit to the identified and deeply distressed sectors of the economy risks arising out of global and domestic economic conditions and geopolitical developments persist. Pandemic effects and worsening domestic economic conditions pose serious threats.

RBIs Financial Sector Development Report

Shows improvement in the Gross NPA ratios and in the capital position of the banks. However, these are pre-Covid positions the actual state of the banks health card will be evident only post-Covid Pandemic, when the bad loans have been adequately provided for and hopefully credit growth picks up as economic activity resumes.

Indian Scenario of the Post Covid World

Changes are already happening. There is a primary push for greater integration and consolidation of the Public Sector Banks and a Kautilya "Matsya Nyay" the big fish, swallow the small fish will follow in the Private Sector ensuring the survival of the fittest.

1. Tranche A in accord with the vision of the Narasimhan Committee report, will consist of Indian banks with domestic and international presence. This process will be augmented by the merger of Public Sector Banks (PSBs).
2. The second Tranche will comprise several mid-sized banking institutions including niche banks with economy-wide presence.
3. The third tranche will encompass smaller private sector banks, small finance banks, regional rural banks and co-operative banks, which specifically cater to the credit requirements of small borrowers in the unorganized sector in rural/local areas.
4. The fourth and last tranche which may reverse the order and occupy first place in the Post Covid-19 years will be of digital players who may act as service providers directly to customers or through banks by acting as their agents or associates.

The reoriented banking system need not be characterized by a continuum of banks. The banking segment need not necessarily have both traditional players with strong customer base and new technology led players.

Timeless Processes

In this scenario the focus has to be on ushering in significant improvements in efficiency and rationalisation of scarce capital to meet the capital adequacy requirements. Investments in technology and skill building must be significant. Banking as a system of settlement of transactions and currency as a store of value will always remain whatever form it takes even if transaction is entirely through cyber widgets. We moved from the Sumerian grain trade to barter to currency we may segue from cash to crypto currency to cyber widgets but the transactional framework the payment for goods and services, the dealings between A and B and the store of value will always remain. The essential processes will be intact as they have been for aeons.

Ultimately, the strength of a banking system or the clone of a banking system whatever form it takes must have ethical practices, depends on the strength of its corporate governance that fosters a robust and ethics-driven compliance culture.

Relevance of the Regulator the present scenario

Returning to the present already questions have been raised on the efficacy of RBIs regulation of the Banking System clearly the RBI needs to reinvent its regulatory responses to stay relevant and ahead of the curve, what had served it well in the past may not work in the future.

Large-scale divergences and frauds observed across banks raises questions on the role and effective utilization of internal control systems within banks to identify areas of emerging risks. To shove off all responsibility on the Boards of the Banks ref RBI Discussion paper on Governance of Banks, hardly exonerates the RBI of its liability to strengthen its own processes of regulation and control or to hive them off altogether in an entirely new institution tasked with regulation and supervision of the Banking system to reinforce the faith of the average man in the Banking system which the assaults of successive frauds has shaken, as at present.

Strengthening Regulation and Supervision

RBI needs to be more nimble and more fast, automate the inspection planning process and cyber incident reporting, and ensure seamless collection and analysis of data so that critical information is available, whenever required. Thematic studies should be across banks and other financial sector entities. Data Analysis, deep dive into data dumps needs to be instituted to have a clearer understanding of the emerging risks and developments in the sector RBI should successfully discern patterns.

There are undeniable gaps in RBI these have to be accepted and addressed with immediacy. In addition to the four pillars of supervision viz. on-site inspection, off-site surveillance, market intelligence and reports of Statutory Auditors (SAs), a fifth pillar of supervision in the form of periodic interaction with all the stakeholders - including statutory auditors, credit rating agencies, credit information companies, mutual funds and banks having large exposures to NBFCs -needs to be effectively taken up.

Digital Delivery Post Covid Response

Many of the relief measures outlined in the Atma Nirbhar package which have been translated into praxis as the seeding of the Bank accounts, Jan Dhan accounts held by women beneficiaries with ₹ 500 over a span of three months and distribution of free grain to the poor on production of aadhar cards have been the result of digital penetration and is the digital dividend which we are receiving. The middle classes and the millenials can still order groceries, books, music and clothes online but it is the poor who can be easily identified and targeted due to the efforts made in the past by putting in place these neural networks of the JAM trinity that would further support rapid digitisation of financial services in India.

Digital Dividend

With inroads into their traditional businesses, banks are expanding into newer areas such as insurance, asset management, brokerage and other services. It is heartening to note that the mindset of banks is changing and they no longer view FinTech firms as disruptive. This change in approach has provided the financial services sector a sense of security. There is evidence that FinTech companies are acting as enablers in the banking ecosystem. Banks are relying on a number of strategies to embrace technological innovation; ranging from investing in FinTech companies and founding their own FinTech subsidiaries, to collaborating with FinTech companies. Banks and non-banks are partnering to offer the combination of trust and innovation to the Indian consumer. This "best of both worlds" approach has resulted in tremendous growth in the number of digital payments, which is expected to continue. These strategies can effectively ensure that banks retain market share, as customers increasingly value more efficient and cost-effective services. Advanced analytics and real-time monitoring of emerging cyber security risks will be critical in detecting potential threats and enabling pre-emptive action.

In the light of these developments, conventional banking is making way for next-generation banking with a focus on digitisation and modernisation. The need for brick and mortar branches is being reviewed continuously as digitisation has literally brought banking to one's fingertips, obviating the need to physically visit a bank branch for most of the banking services.

India-digital Payments

The movement towards digital payments has also been facilitated by introduction of fast payment systems, such as Immediate Payment Service (IMPS) and Unified Payment Interface (UPI), which provide immediate credit to beneficiaries and are available round the clock. The extent of digital penetration can be gauged from the fact that, each day on an average, the payment systems in India process more than 10 crore transactions of nearly INR 6 lakh crore. Today, digital payments account for around 97 percent of daily payment system transactions in terms of volume. This has been made possible with an accelerated growth of over 50 percent in the volume of digital payment transactions in the last five years.

National Electronic Funds Transfer (NEFT) is in operation by the RBI on a 24x7 basis. The Bank for International Settlements (BIS), in a recently published paper, has indicated that the UPI framework of India can become an international model to facilitate quick and seamless payments not only within countries but even across countries. The National Payments Corporation of India (NPCI) has also decided to set up a subsidiary to focus on taking the UPI model to other countries which will help enhance global outreach of India's payment systems. Pan-India New Umbrella Entity (NUE) for retail payment systems is needed.

Cooperative Banking System

From June 25th, following the cabinet decision, 1,482 urban cooperative banks and 58 multi-state cooperative banks will come under the central bank's oversight, which would mean tighter supervision. RBI's powers on scheduled banks would be hence applicable on cooperative banks as well. One reason why cooperative banks failed so often is their small capital base. RBI's supervision of cooperative banks is not as stringent as that of commercial banks. Typically, the state government audits cooperative banks while RBI inspects their books once a year. They (cooperative banks) actually play a very important role in the rural areas. But, at the same time, if you are taking deposits, you need to be responsible to the customer also. So, those norms will change through the Banking Regulation Act to make it far more robust in terms of regulation:

1. RBI to have better control over Cooperative Banks.
2. Move to ensure professionalism and effective corporate Governance.
3. RBI has powers to supersede the Board and alter the Management if Cooperative Bank fails. Prior to this the RBI had to request the State Government to change the management.
4. This will protect the interests of depositors. DICGC cover upto 5 lac will be available to them.
5. The Banks will be subject to the stringency of RBI Audits.
6. The approval of the RBI will be essential before the appointment of the CEO this is expected to increase professionalism and nip the tendency of politicization in CEO appointments and of gaming the system.
7. Dual Regulation of RBI and the Registrar of Cooperative Banks did not work several instances of frauds came to light and the spectacular failure of the Punjab and Maharashtra Cooperative Bank brought to the fore the frailties in the system.
8. Urban Cooperative Banks and Multi State Cooperative Banks 1540 in number with a depositor base 8.6 crore and savings of 4.84 lakh crore.

RBI has been given regulatory powers in respect of Urban Co-operative Banks, on par with those over banking companies, amendments in the Banking Regulation Act, 1949.

RBI has put in place stress-testing framework for urban cooperative banks (UCBs). It also acts as an early warning system for co-operative banks with the purpose of timely identification of weak banks for appropriate action. This is a shift from reactive to pro-active supervisory approach, intended to ensure surveillance of vulnerabilities in UCBs on an ongoing basis. Moreover, as on December 31, 2019, more than 90 percent of these banks are now on Core Banking Solution (CBS), although efforts are still required to standardize the solutions and have robust set of internal controls implemented in the CBS for improved outcomes. The CAMELS (Capital, Asset Quality, Management, Earnings, Liquidity and Systems and Control) supervisory rating methodology for UCBs has been comprehensively revised. RBI has taken steps to bring UCBs under the CRILC reporting framework and issued draft guidelines on exposure norms to mitigate credit concentration risk and enhancement in Priority Sector lending targets to further financial inclusion. To improve governance, guidelines on constitution of Board of Management (BOM) for UCBs with deposit size of ₹ 100 crores and above while making it voluntary for adoption by other smaller UCBs.

Further Looking Ahead

The changing scenario of the banking industry will necessarily

1. Require a regulatory and supervisory regime of stringency with increased intensity and tech-enabled supervision of banks with a regulator who consciously stays ahead of the curve.
2. The challenge for banks is to make the best use of technology and innovation to bring down intermediation costs while protecting their bottom lines.
3. Artificial Intelligence (AI), Machine Learning (ML) and Big Data are fairly central to financial services innovation. They assist/help in detection of malfeasance/misfeasance identification of better ways of monitoring use of funds by

borrowers, track suspicious transactions, etc. by processing large datasets.

4. Proportionality Ensure that new innovations in banking sector serve the customer by reducing the cost of financial services and enhancing the range and access to products in a manner that is safe.

The Pandemic will compel a changed economic environment. To stay relevant Banks will need to reformulate, business strategies, innovate customer centric segmented products, one size fits all will no longer do. They will have to customize products for different age brackets to meet changing tastes and life cycle needs. The possibilities are enormous. The Banks will also have to change to adapt to a new business paradigm in the Post Covid-19 world.

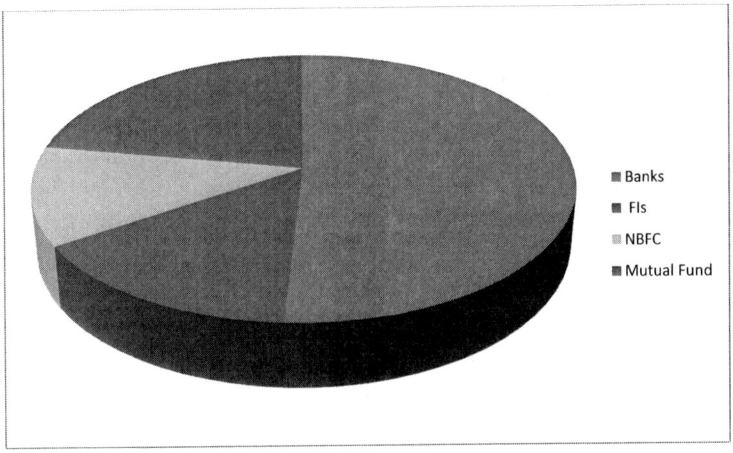

The government wants stronger and well capitalized institutions, able to underpin an economic trajectory of high growth.

Restructuring and Consolidation of the Banking Sector is essential to enhance competitiveness:

(1) Vijaya + Dena Bank merge with the Bank of Baroda

(2) Oriental Bank of Commerce + United Bank of India with Punjab National Bank making it the second largest lender

(3) Syndicate + Canara

(4) Andhra + Corporation Bank with Union Bank of India

(5) Allahabad Bank + Indian Bank

(a) IDBI has been taken over by LIC

(b) SBI and its subsidiaries have already merged.

This is not privatization by stealth. Financial Sector has seen the moves to amalgamation of Public Sector Banks followed by fresh capitalization of these Banks.

Critics carp that the recapitalization, is just enough to meet the Capital Conservation Buffer which enables provision coverage for Non Performing Assets. Injection of 70,000 crore by strengthening the Capital position of some of these Banks has enabled them to transit from the Prompt Corrective Action regimen of the RBI Pre-January 2019. Eleven PSBS were in the PCA regimen however, Fresh Capital Infusion and Systemic Structural Improvements, CET-1, CRAR/NPA less than 6% and adequate Capital Conservation Buffers. Since then BOI, BOM, Allahabad Bank, Corporation Bank and Dhanalaxmi have moved out of the PCA frame. Recapitalisation is a necessity as access to Capital Markets raising resources through Public Issue constrained due to Volatile Market conditions. The Insolvency and Bankruptcy Code moves as slowly as its predecessors the SARFEISI does not lend comfort to expeditious resolution to deleverage the Banks Balance Sheets from the overhang of Stressed Assets, slippages are increasing. They are trammeled by stressed assets and fresh slippages 7.27 crore may rise to 13.2 crore by September. The Banks are trammeled by a severe lack of Board Level leadership and governance; there should be greater rigour in the selection of Directors on the Boards of these Banks. Professional capability and expertise should also be coupled with the ability to exercise judgment and to influence Board Level Decisions, with Fairness, Accountability Independence and Transparency. Efficiency in allocation of resources is essential. Frauds happen because the internal culture is not strong; the rules are there but are given the go by. Lapses in Internal risk governance, non-adherence to regulatory guidelines, ignoring early warning signals, market intelligence units which do not have an ear to the ground, compromised internal systems. All these need immediate redress if these Banks are to emerge as strong and sustainable institutions which do not look for perpetual capita support and succor from the government. They are also faced by technological challenges they have to adapt to the new technological autobahn and swiftly respond to customer needs. Technology is going to be the key driver of business growth. Their deposit share has dropped from 78 to 61% their asset share has declined from 76% to 66%. They have lost significant market share to the new Private Sector Banks which promise higher interest rates on savings and term deposits, though this considerably increases Private Banks cost of deposits and Credit share to the new technology driven entrants to the credit market, peer to peer lenders, vulnerability of the NBFC sector has not helped PSBs reclaim credit share as there are several new banks and digital modes of lending in the fray which offer finer rates. They face loss of deposit, credit and overall market share.

Their risk weighted assets and NPAs remain high despite the 2.4 lac crore capital injection they have received in the recent past. Public Sector Banks commitments to the Government on Priority Sector loans etc. are also high. Internally their operating expenses are increasing. Trade unions remain strong and will contribute to the merger woes on issues of cultural mesh and a perceived lack of promotion opportunities as a result of mergers.

Yet the public perception views Public Sector Banks as safe compared to Private Bank as Yes Bank. Yes Bank despite change in management does not inspire any confidence in Investors, Savers or borrowers. It is a capital starved Bank, the quantum of capital it requires is expected to increase earlier estimates of 1.2 billion to 2.0 billion in November 19, its capital rising, liquidity, funding profile and asset need quality close watch. NPAs are high; solvency profile weakening. It has been subject to rating downgrades. Moodys has given it a rating of Outlook negative. Ability to raise capital will require regulatory approvals from RBI and be subject to the rigour of the regulators due diligence on Investors. None of these factors inspire confidence in potential Investors.

The other Private Sector Banks as HDFC, Kotak Mahindra have shown strong core growth. HDFC has a market capitalization of

4.6 trillion and Kotak Mahindra of 1.92 trillion and strong retail lending MSME franchise and a strong corporate loan book.

India's Financial Sector is characterized by a dominance of Public Sector Banks; they score on large branch networks, brand image, public confidence that they are too big to fail. They would be bailed out, recapitalized by the government therefore they are "Safe". These assumptions are also correct however this does not detract from the fact that the operating environment is getting tougher, that there is a tradeoff between efficiency and improved financial and operational performance, the one is no longer a corollary of the other.

The Government wants stronger and well capitalized institutions, able to underpin an economic trajectory of high growth.

After a near brush with collapse, in a first, the Private Bank was bailed out by a clutch of Investors in a consortium led by the SBI. The Cabinet approved the reconstruction scheme proposed by the RBI under section 44 of the Banking Regulation Act for the tottering private sector. Eight financial Institutions invested committed 12,550 crore in Capita to address the Banks immediate needs. Yes Bank, HDFC (Housing Development Finance Corporation), ICICI, Kotak Mahindrs Bank, RK Damani, Jhunjhunwala and the Azim Premji Trust which invested 12000 crore with a share of 3% of which SBI as the leader invested 6050 crore. ICICI Bank will invest 1000 crore, AXIS Bank and HDFC 600 each, Kotak Mahindra Bank will contribute ₹ 500 crore, Bandhan Bank will invest ₹ 300 crore and IDFC Bank will put in ₹ 250 crore.

The other Private Sector Banks as HDFC, Kotak Mahindra have shown strong core growth. HDFC has a market capitalization of 4.6 trillion and Kotak Mahindra of 1.92 trillion and strong retail lending MSME franchise and a strong corporate loan book. The Yes Bank marks a first in other ways too, it is being bailed by a consortium unlike previous mergers which were straightforward amalgamations as the merger of the Global Trust Bank with the Oriental Bank of Commerce or that of the United Western Bank with the IDBI Bank or the merger of Bank of Rajasthan with the ICICI bank even before a moratorium was announced. As per rules one Bank cannot hold more than 10% in another Bank. SBI breached that limit and was

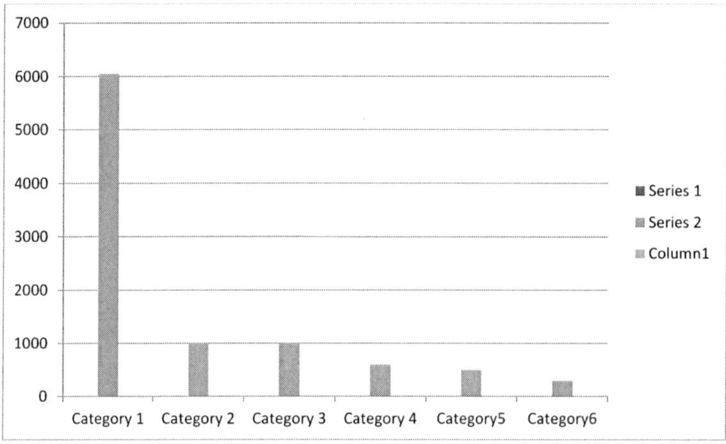

also permitted to hold 26% committed for three years. SBI has been exempted from the rule that no bank can hold equity of more than 26% in another Bank. The Yes Bank episode considerably dented confidence in the Private Sector Banks as a whole.

The Government

The operating environment for Banks is tough in an environment of slowing global growth which also impinges on domestic credit growth. This leads to a study of Banking Sector reforms.

The history of Banking Sector reforms. Narasimham Committee was set up in 1991 with a wide sweep a catch all mandate to examine all aspects related to structure organization and functions of the Banking system, to morph the gargantuan and perceived to be slothful Banking system

Banking Sector Reforms

Phase I Recommendations of the Narasimham Committee I

Deregulation of the Interest Rate Structure

Progressive reduction in Pre-emptive reserves

Liberalisation of the Branch Expansion Policy

Introduction of Prudential norms to ensure Capital adequacy, correct income recognition classification of assets based on their quality and provisioning requirements. Provisioning against bad and doubtful debts

Decreasing the emphasis on directed credit phasing out concessional rates of interest for the priority sector

Deregulation of norms for private sector and foreign banks

Enabling public and private sector banks to access the capital market

Setting up the Asset Reconstruction Fund

Establishment of Debt Recovery Tribunals

Freedom to appoint the chief executives and officers of the Bank

Changes in the constitution of the Board

NBFCs brought under regulatory ambit.

The second wave of reforms came with the second Narasimham Committee of 1998. This Committee tried to ensure that Indian Banking standards on Bank Solvency and Bank Capital are on par with International Standards set by the Basle Committee.

Narasimham Committee Report II - 1998

In 1998, the government appointed yet another committee under the chairmanship of Mr Narasimham. It is better known as the Banking Sector Committee. It was told to review the banking reform progress and design a programme for further strengthening the financial system of India. The committee focused on various areas such as capital adequacy, bank mergers, bank legislation, etc.

It submitted its report to the Government in April 1998 with the following recommendations.

1. **Strengthening Banks in India:** The committee considered the stronger banking system in the context of the Current Account Convertibility 'CAC'. It thought that Indian banks must be capable of handling problems regarding domestic liquidity and exchange rate management in the light of CAC. Thus, it recommended the merger of strong banks which will have 'multiplier effect' on the industry.
2. **Narrow Banking:** Those days many public sector banks were facing a problem of the Non-performing assets (NPAs).

Some of them had NPAs were as high as 20 percent of their assets. Thus, for successful rehabilitation of these banks, it recommended 'Narrow Banking Concept' where weak banks will be allowed to place their funds only in the short term and risk-free assets.

3. **Capital Adequacy Ratio:** In order to improve the inherent strength of the Indian banking system the committee recommended that the Government should raise the prescribed capital adequacy norms. This will further improve their credit absorption capacity. Currently, the capital adequacy ratio for Indian banks is at 9 percent (PSB's 12 percent).
4. **Bank ownership:** As it had earlier mentioned the freedom for banks in its working and bank autonomy, it felt that the government control over the banks in the form of management and ownership and bank autonomy does not go hand-in-hand and thus it recommended a review of functions of boards and enabled them to adopt professional corporate strategy.
5. **Review of banking laws:** The committee considered that there was an urgent need for reviewing and amending main laws governing Indian Banking Industry like RBI Act, Banking Regulation Act, State Bank of India Act, Bank Nationalisation Act, etc. This upgradation will bring them in line with the present needs of the banking sector in India.

Apart from these major recommendations, the committee has also recommended faster computerization, technology up-gradation, training of staff, depoliticizing of banks, professionalism in banking, reviewing bank recruit.

The PJ Nayak Committee was set up in 2014

Its major recommendations were

1. Government to reduce its stake in Public Sector Banks to 51% eventually leading to a privatization of Public Sector Banks.

2. The reduction will take the Public Sector Banks out of vigilance tyranny, there seems to be a commonly held view that the Public Sector Banks are not as swift as Private Sector Banks to cash in on new business opportunities. They live in a fear psychosis which induces decision paralysis. They fear that their decisions will be questioned and they will be hauled up by the courts raked over the coals by the Central Vigilance Commission and the Central Bureau of Investigation, the dreaded CBI will subject them to grilling. There may be some truth in this argument but it is not the whole truth.
3. It recommended the establishment of a two tier holding Company a Bank Investment Company which would be managed entirely by Investors and later by Banks Board.
4. The establishment of a Bank Board Bureau which would be responsible for the appointment of Chairman and Managing Directors of Banks.
5. The post of Chairman and Managing Director be split and a fixed term of five years for the Banks Chairman and three years for a whole time Director.

Essentially it recommended privatization of Public Sector Banks and a wide range of Governance reforms.

Recapitalization of Banks

The Union Government has recapitalized the Public Sector Banks to the extent of ₹ 70,000 crore to strengthen and enhance their lending capacity. Recapitalisation will take place in two tranches in the first the Banks will subscribe to bonds floated by the Government and in the second Government will infuse money into the Public Sector Banks from FY 15 to FY 19 the Public Sector Banks have been recapitalized to the extent of 3.19 trillion with an infusion of 2.5 trillion by the Government and the mobilization of over ₹ 66000 crore by PSBs themselves BOI, ₹ 30,399, PNB ₹ 24,342, SBI, ₹ 22,844, IDBI ₹ 16,600, UCO, ₹ 15773, IOB, ₹ 15,317, Corporation Bank ₹ 15,193, Allahabad Bank, ₹ 14,984, Central Bank of India ₹ 13,682, Bank of Baroda ₹ 13,463.

The recapitalization amount is expected to take care of the credit growth of 15% apart from the regulatory requirement. Capital infusion by the Government will help the banks to move out of the Prompt Corrective Action framework, it would help the flow of credit to the economy though as Moody's put it, it would add to governments debt.

If we are to double credit GDP ratio to 100% Governance reforms in Public Sector Banks along with strengthening regulation and supervision of RBI.

A sustainable way, to raise the credit to GDP ratio through five measures:

1. Greater penetration and larger Number of Banks. India is a large country. In Maharashtra each bank office serves 9,515 people, compared to the All India average of 9,280 people. In Goa, each branch serves only 2,178 people while in Manipur 20,696 people have to make do with one bank branch and in Bihar including Jharkhand 15,278 people are served with one bank branch. While we do need greater penetration the larger question is how efficacious is digital penetration. How much trust do the common people repose in the Bank in a box of the business correspondent. Have small finance banks and Payments banks made any in-roads at all in the rural areas. The spread of branches and the consolidation at the top should not be seen as contradictory. The consolidation at the top will create larger banking behemoths and may actually serve to increase the branch network with stronger banks.
2. Accountability, the lack of effective corporate governance continue to trammel the Bank Boards. In the Public Sector Banks, the influence of Government is overweening and impacts the ability to take judicious commercial decisions. The Government is the dominant shareholder in the Public Sector Banks. Thus, the shareholders are strong and Boards and Bank Managements are weak. In the Private Sector Banks, the Promoters and CEOs of the Banks are all powerful, the Boards and shareholders are weak in either

case, corporate governance is impaired.

3. In the case of the Public Sector Banks the fear of CBI, Courts, CVC makes it increasingly difficult to take a decision, while in the case of Promoter led Private Sector Banks the fear is that they will bet the bank in a hurry to grow exponentially.
4. RBI needs to strengthen Regulation and Supervision so that episodes like the PMC Bank and Yes Bank do not recur.
5. Encourage participation of Non Bank players. UPI is an example of success. It was a success due to the active role of non-bank players.

The Net Financial Assets of Households have risen on decline of borrowings from Banks as per RBI data. Though the Banks are flush with funds, in the grim shadow of a recession and in a declining economy bleak scenario firms are postponing their spending and expansion decisions just as households are postponing consumption spends. The rainy day is upon us.

Financial Assets and Liabilities of Households

Year	*2017-18*	*2018-19*	*2019-20*
Net Financial Assets (A-B)	13.29(7.7)	13.73(7.2)	15.62(7.7)
A. Gross Financial Assets	20.6(12.0)	21.23(11.1)	21.63(10.6)
B. Financial Liabilities	7.31(4.2)	7.5 (3.9)	6.01(2.9)
Amount in lakh crores			
Figures in parenthesis as percent to GDP			

RBI data as per the Quarterly Estimates of Households Financial Assets and Liabilities reflects that in March 2020 end of the financial year, the net financial assets defined as Gross Financial Assets - borrowings increased from ₹ 13.73 lakh crore in Financial Year 2019 to 15.62 lakh crore last financial year while the gross financial assets rose from ₹ 21.23 lakh crore to ₹ 21.63 lakh crore last year the financial liabilities witnessed a sharp decline from ₹ 7.5 lakh crore to ₹ 6.01 lakh crore contributing thereby to the rise in the net financial assets. This has occurred as households are borrowing less and saving more with banks which points to a significant slowdown in the economy in 2019-20, this sharp decline in the share of borrowings from the Banking sector in total liabilities during 2019-20 reflects the economic slow down and the risk aversion of Banks currency and deposits with Banks account for 66% of total financial assets followed by Insurance funds and Mutual funds COVID related uncertainties have led to an outflow from mutual funds and a flight to currency holdings moreover decline in construction activity will also increase the shift from physical to financial assets. While the household sector is the most self-reliant and sustainable sector for financing the Indian Economy its role is critical aligning with the policy effort to lift the Indian economy from the grip of slowdown and the life threatening Covid-19 pandemic. SBI Chairman speaking at a CII conclave pointed out that "I hear a lot about risk aversion of the bankers but there is a lot of risk aversion on the side of the borrowers too, I have money but there are no takers for that money." RBI data reflects that credit growth has fallen nearly 50% to 6% year-on-year which is fairly dire.

CRISIL estimates credit growth for the fiscal year could be 0-1%, about 800 basis points lower than the pre-pandemic estimates of 8-9% CRISIL says that "This crisis is unprecedented and so will its economic fall out be such as lower capex demand as well as lower discretionary spends, to name some which will slow down credit off take significantly across segments in the current fiscal year. The corporate loan portfolio is expected to be the worst hit." The visible signs are the steep reduction in the factory output data to 55.5% contraction in the Index of Industrial Production the worst among the G-20 countries. Credit demand is thin.

It is expected that there will be demand for credit from MSMEs and NBFCs and the Agriculture sector, this is only half of the story the second half of it is dire. When the moratorium ends and banks are expected to square off their losses they anticipate a pile up in the bad loans. The Banks are already burdened with NPAs. The NPAs are in the Retail, Farming and MSME sector

Column 1 is the December 2019 position

Column 2 is the base scenario

Column 3 is the Stress case scenario

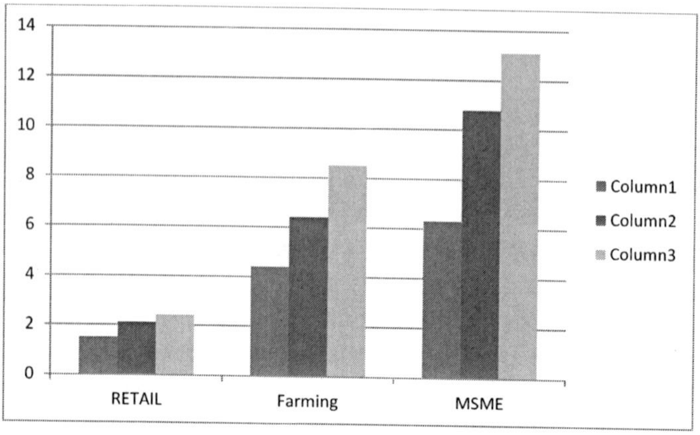

Not surprisingly banks are wary of overextension or of plain vanilla lending to particular sectors as the Hospitality, Airlines and Tourism sectors as these have suffered the most due to Covid, the lockdown and its related constraints.

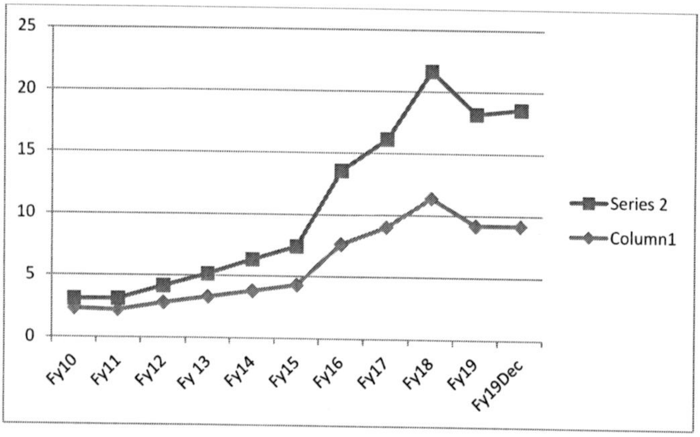

This reflects the exponential increase in the NPA position. In the coming months the key cost ratios of banks will be stressed and will compel the banks to rethink their fixed cost strategy.

Higher NPA leads to following adverse impact on Economy

Depositors do not get rightful returns and many times may lose uninsured deposits. Banks may begin charging higher interest rates on some products to compensate Non-Higher NPA leads to following adverse impact on Economy:

1. Depositors do not get rightful returns and many times may lose uninsured deposits. Banks may begin charging higher interest rates on some products to compensate Non- performing loan losses.
2. Bank shareholders are adversely affected.
3. Bad loans imply redirecting of funds from good projects to bad ones. Hence, the economy suffers due to loss of good projects and failure of bad investments.
4. When bank do not get loan repayment or interest payments, liquidity problems may ensue:
    1. Performing loan losses
    2. Bank shareholders are adversely affected
    3. Bad loans imply redirecting of funds from good projects to bad ones. Hence, the economy suffers due to loss of good projects and failure of bad investments
    4. When bank do not get loan repayment or interest payments, liquidity problems may ensue
        1. **Five sectors:** Textile, aviation, mining, infrastructure, Real estate contributes to most of the NPA, since most of the loan given in these sector are by PSB, **they account for most of the NPA.**
        2. **Public Sector banks provide around 80% of the credit to industries** and it is this part of the credit distribution that forms a great chunk of NPA. Last year, when kingfisher was marred in financial crisis, SBI provided it huge amount of loan which it is not able to recover from it.
        3. Less Professional management.
        4. Political Pressure and interference forces PSB to lend to not so commercially sounds project.

1. **Government has launched Mission Indradhanush** to make the working of public sector bank more transparent and professional in order to curb the menace of NPA in future.
2. Government has also proposed to introduce **Bankruptcy code** which will make it easier for banks to recover the loans from the debtors.
3. **RBI introduced number of measures in last few years which include:**
4. Tightening the Corporate Debt Restructuring (CDR) mechanism,
5. **Setting up a Joint Lenders' Forum,** prodding banks to disclose the real picture of bad loans, asking them to increase provisioning for stressed assets,
6. Introducing a 5:25 scheme where loans are to be amortized over 25 years with refinancing option after every five years, and
    1. **Improving credit risk management-** This includes credit appraisal, credit monitoring, and efficient system of fixing accountability and analyzing trends in group leverage to which the borrowing firm belongs to.
    2. **Sources/structure of equity capital-** Banks need to see that promoter's contribution is funded through equity and not debt.
    3. Banks should conduct necessary **sensitivity analysis and contingency planning** while appraising the projects and it should built adequate safeguards against such external factors.
    4. **Strengthen credit monitoring-** Develop an early warning mechanism and comprehensive MIS (Management information system) can play an important role in it. MIS must enable timely detection of problem accounts, flag early signs of delinquencies and facilitate timely information to management on these aspects.

5. **Enforce accountability-** Till now lower rung officials considered accountable even though loaning decisions are taken at higher level. Thus, sanction official should also share the burden of responsibility.
6. **Restructured accounts** should treated as non-performing and technical write offs where banks remove NPA's from their balance sheets. Permanently should be dispensed with.
7. **Address corporate governance issues in PSB-** This includes explicit fit and proper criteria for appointment of top executives and instituting system of an open market wide search for Chairman:
    1. Hitherto India was lacking the legal and institutional machinery for dealing with debt defaults as per the global standards.
    2. The recovery proceedings by creditors, either through the Contract Act or through special laws such as the Recovery of Debts **due to Banks and Financial Institutions Act, 1993** and the Securitisation and Reconstruction of Financial Assets and Enforcement of Security Interest Act, 2002, has not had desired outcomes.
    3. **Similarly, action through the Sick Industrial Companies (Special Provisions) Act, 1985 (SICA) and the winding up provisions of the Companies Act, 1956 have neither been able to aid recovery for lenders nor restructuring of firms.**
    4. **Laws dealing with individual insolvency, the Presidency Towns Insolvency Act, 1909 and the Provincial Insolvency Act, 1920, were almost a century old.** This has hampered the confidence of the lender and development of the credit markets in India. Resultantly, credit by banks is the largest component of the credit market in India and corporate bond market has not yet developed to the desired level.

1. **The Code creates time-bound processes for insolvency** resolution of companies and individuals. These processes will be completed within 180 days. If insolvency cannot be resolved, the assets of the borrowers may be sold to repay creditors.
2. **The resolution processes will be conducted by licenced insolvency professionals (IPs).** These IPs will be members of insolvency professional agencies (IPAs). IPAs will also furnish performance bonds equal to the assets of a company under insolvency resolution.
3. **Information utilities (IUs)** will be established to collect, collate and disseminate financial information to facilitate insolvency resolution.
4. **The National Company Law Tribunal (NCLT)** will adjudicate insolvency resolution for companies. The Debt Recovery Tribunal (DRT) will adjudicate insolvency resolution for individuals.
5. **The Insolvency and Bankruptcy Board of India will be set up to regulate functioning of IPs, IPAs and IUs.**
    1. **Plus points the new law aims to consolidate the laws relating to insolvency of companies and limited liability entities** (including limited liability partnerships and other entities with limited liability), unlimited liability partnerships and individuals. Presently contained in a number of legislations, into a single legislation and provide for their reorganization and resolution in a time bound manner for maximization of value of their assets.
    2. **Such consolidation will provide for a greater clarity** in law and facilitate the application of consistent and coherent provisions to different stakeholders affected by business failure or inability to pay debt.
    3. **This law will thus promote entrepreneurship,** availability of credit and balance the interest of all stakeholders.

4. **It is true that some business ventures will always fail, but such failures will be handled rapidly and swiftly. Entrepreneurs and lenders will be able to move on, instead of being bogged down with decisions taken in the past.**
5. **The Code empowers the operational creditors** (workmen, suppliers etc.) also to initiate the insolvency resolution process upon non-payment of dues. In order to develop the credit market in India, in case of liquidation, financial debts owed to unsecured creditors have been kept above the government's dues in the list of priorities (waterfall).
6. **Facilitating early resolution and exit is as important as facilitating investment.**
7. The essential idea of the new law is that when a corporate entity defaults on its debt, control shifts from the shareholders/ promoters to a committee of creditors, who have 180 days (extendable by 90 days in deserving cases) to evaluate proposals from various players about resuscitating the company or taking it into liquidation.
8. **When decisions are taken in a time-bound manner,** there is a greater chance that the corporate entity can be saved as a going concern, and the productive resources of the economy (labour and capital) can be put to the best use. This is in complete departure from SICA regime where there were delays leading to destruction of the value of the firm.
9. **The Code separates commercial aspects of the insolvency proceedings from judicial aspects.**
10. While Insolvency Professionals (IPs) will deal with commercial aspects such as management of the affairs of the corporate debtor, facilitating formation of committee of creditors, organising their meetings, examination of the resolution plan, etc.
11. **Judicial issues will be handled by proposed Adjudicating Authorities** (National Company Law

Tribunal / Debt Recovery Tribunal). One more important institution created under the Code is the 'Information Utility' which would store financial information and data and terms of lending in electronic databases. This would eliminate delays and disputes about facts when default does take place.

12. The Code also provides a fast track insolvency resolution process for corporates and LLPs. This will be an enabler for start-ups and small and medium enterprises (SMEs) to complete the resolution process in 90 days (extendable to 45 days in deserving cases).
13. **The Code also addresses the important issue relating to cross border insolvency by providing the enabling mechanism on the subject.** The government, at an appropriate time, will come out with a detailed framework for cross border insolvency.
    1. **In relation to corporate persons, the Code looks to wrap up the game in 180 days.**
    2. It warrants a notice of dispute to be issued followed by a response period of 10 days for the corporate debtor, failing which the creditor is entitled to file an insolvency application before the National Company Law Tribunal (NCLT).
    3. **Within 14 days from filing, the application must be admitted. Upon admission, the moratorium period (freezing of bank accounts, prohibition on foreclosures in relation to financial debts, etc.)** commences.
    4. At this stage, the existing management of the company loses complete control and all powers vest with an interim resolution professional, who has merely 30 days to put together all the relevant information and call for a meeting of the financial creditors.
    5. **Once the financial creditors meet, they must appoint a resolution professional who will put**

together an information memorandum of the company that forms the basis for a resolution applicant to propose a resolution plan for the company.

6. **The Code fails to define a resolution applicant.** All such resolution plans are placed before the financial creditors. When at least 75% of the financial creditors approve, the plan is implemented by way of an order by the NCLT. If the financial creditors fail to arrive at a consensus, the default plan is to liquidate the company.
7. **The Code rides substantially on the unquestionable word of the creditors.** Neither does the corporate debtor have an opportunity to put forth his/her case nor is there any scope of discretion provided to the adjudicating authority itself.
8. At various stages — of admission of the insolvency proceedings, of appointing the insolvency professional, of finalising the resolution plan — **the Code fails to provide any opportunity to the corporate debtor to make a representation, at the very least.**
9. In this manner, the Code ignores rights enshrined in the Constitution. **(In Maneka Gandhi v. Union of India, 1978, the Supreme Court observed that it is the duty of the authority to give reasonable opportunity to be heard, even where there is no specific provision for showing cause when a proposed action affects the rights of the individual.)**
10. The Code is also deficient in providing a yardstick for the qualification of the interim and of the final insolvency resolution professionals. It allows for any person to access the information memorandum put together by the insolvency professional without restricting competitors or imposing any confidentiality obligations.

11. This allows for any person to access proprietary information of the corporate debtor and misuse the same, given that there is no law protecting confidentiality and vitiates the fundamental right to business under Article 19(1)(g).
12. The Code prohibits withdrawal of the application once the same has been admitted.
13. This means that there is no scope whatsoever for settlement.
14. This is despite the recent ruling of the Supreme Court in Lokhandwala Kataria Construction (P) Ltd. v. Nisus Finance and Investment Managers LLP (2017), wherein a settlement proposal was taken on record and the appeal was disposed of. However, this cannot be held as a precedent.
15. Further, the unrestricted access of any person without mandatory contractual obligations in relation to confidentiality vitiates the fundamental right to business under Article 19(1)(g).
16. Time-bound insolvency resolution will require establishment of several new entities. Also, given the pendency and disposal rate of DRTs, their current capacity may be inadequate to take up the additional role.
17. IPAs, regulated by the Board, will be created for regulating the functioning of IPs. This approach of having regulated entities further regulate professionals may be contrary to the current practice of regulating licenced professionals. Further, requiring a high value of performance bond may deter the formation of IPAs.
18. The Code provides an order of priority to distribute assets during liquidation. It is unclear why: (i) secured creditors will receive their entire outstanding amount, rather than up to their collateral value, (ii) unsecured creditors have priority over trade creditors, and

(iii) government dues will be repaid after unsecured creditors.

19. The Code provides for the creation of multiple IUs. However, it does not specify that full information about a company will be accessible through a single query from any IU. This may lead to financial information being scattered across these IUs.
20. The Code creates an Insolvency and Bankruptcy Fund. However, it does not specify the manner in which the Fund will be used.

The Insolvency and Bankruptcy Code is a comprehensive and systemic reform, which will give a quantum leap to the functioning of the credit market. It would take India from among relatively weak insolvency regimes to becoming one of the world's best insolvency regimes. It lays the foundations for the development of the corporate bond market, which would finance the infrastructure projects of the future. The passing of this Code and implementation of the same was expected to give a big boost to ease of doing business in India. This did not happen the processes of settlement remained tardy and protracted and did not live up to what was expected of them. Due to Covid Pandemic the code has been suspended for six months. This does not send a very positive message. Many a time, to see through to the future, looking back at the past provides insights that are of much help. With that limited objective, wade back a little to the past for the sake of contextualising our discussion. In 1967, credit to agriculture constituted only 2.2 percent of the total advances of the Scheduled Commercial Banks in sharp contrast to industry which constituted 64.3 percent. Five cities in the country, *viz.*, Ahmedabad, Mumbai, Delhi, Kolkata and Chennai accounted for around 44 percent of the bank deposits and 60 percent of the outstanding bank credit in1969. This led to the widespread political perception that, left to themselves, the private sector banks were not sufficiently aware of their larger responsibilities towards society. The solutions that the policy-makers thought of at that time included exerting various degrees of control over the banking system, which ultimately culminated in the decision to nationalise 14 private sector banks in 1969, followed by the nationalisation of six more private sector banks in 1980. The impact of the decision to nationalise banks has been succinctly summarised in the History of RBI, Volume III: "*....at the time of nationalisation as many as 617 towns out of 2,700 in the country were not covered by commercial banks. And, even worse, out of about 600,000 villages, hardly 5,000 had banks. The spread, too, was uneven......*"

Current Challenges and the Role of Exogenous Factors

Challenges faced by the banks today, many of which are a result of how various exogenous factors have played out over the years. Everyone concerned should realize that banks are in the business of taking bonafide risks. This means that out of a host of exposures which a bank chooses to take, a few may go bad. The PSBs, which have been used as vehicles to further the development agenda of the Government, had to achieve and maximise multiple objectives. The high growth phase prior to the GFC (2008) was aided by bank credit to a large extent, mostly by PSBs, leading to risk build ups in the balance sheet of the lenders. In particular, bank credit to infrastructure sector increased at an unprecedented rate. This exposed the PSBs to the travails of the infrastructure sector, which materialised significantly in the post-crisis years.

Further, the tail end of the above high growth period in advances to infrastructure coincided with a period of slowdown in economic growth and tightening of environmental clearances. Also, the transformation of major term lending institutions into universal banks/NBFCs led to commercial banks becoming the primary source of longterm debt financing to projects in infrastructure and core industries. An immediate consequence of these circumstances was that it led to a spurt in the level of 'restructured standard assets', *i.e.*, assets which were restructured without being downgraded as non-performing assets (NPAs). Eventually, most of the restructured assets which were allowed to be classified as 'standard' became NPAs as the restructuring packages proved to be unviable. Inadequate credit assessment by banks and governance issues also played their due part in the risk build-up.

The increase in NPAs was significantly higher in PSBs as compared to their private and foreign counterparts. PSBs, probably to fulfil the additional social objective of their mandate, had taken higher exposure in some of the critical sectors of the economy such as mining, iron and steel, and infrastructure. NPA levels in these sectors shot up as all these sectors suffered external shocks leading to the respective stress - mining and energy was hit by the cancellation of allocation of coal blocks; iron and steel sector faced cost pressures due to dumping of cheaper steel from China; telecommunications sector underwent a disruption in the form of cancellation of 2G spectrum allotment; and the construction sector was marred by delays in obtaining necessary government approvals, in particular environmental clearances.

Shocks in the form of debt waivers/moratoriums and payment issues of DISCOMs also meant significant costs to the fisc and also affected the health of the banking sector as well as the credit culture. Interestingly, data put together by the Indian Banks Association shows that of the 10 states that announced debt waiver schemes since 2017, only three states have reimbursed almost completely as promised. Thus, it is imperative that write-off amounts are reimbursed to the banks and DISCOM payments are made in a time bound manner, so as to improve the health of banks and their capacity to lend in subsequent years.

Corporate Governance - The Elephant in the Room

Their governance could easily be identified as a central concern. In fact, many of the problems that currently seem to affect the PSBs such as the elevated levels of NPA, capital shortfalls, frauds and inadequate risk management can mostly be attributed to the manifestation of underlying corporate governance issues. The role of independent Boards in fostering a compliance culture by establishing the proper systems of control, audit and distinct reporting of business and risk management has been found wanting in some PSBs leading to build-up of NPAs. Also, the understanding of risks from a business perspective by the Boards in some banks has been inadequate due to skill gap and, competency issues. The fact remains that a strong corporate governance culture, with a focus on transparency and accountability, has to percolate from a strong Board which sets the example by leading.

Governance issues in Private Sector Banks (PVBs) which originate from altogether different set of concerns. The issues here mainly relate to incentive structure of their managements, quality of audits and compliance and also functioning of Audit and Risk Management Committees. The Reserve Bank has recently issued guidelines for compensation in private sector banks which include specification of minimum variable pay component and clawback arrangements, among others.

Resolution of Stressed Assets

Apart from governance, one of the biggest challenges faced by the PSBs, and the banking system in general, is the resolution of stressed assets. For a long time, India did not have a bankruptcy law in place, and hence the Reserve Bank introduced various restructuring frameworks which were designed to emulate the desirable attributes of a bankruptcy law. The enactment of the Insolvency and Bankruptcy Code, 2016 (IBC) has been a game changer in this regard. Despite the impression that IBC has been marred with numerous litigations leading to delays in resolution, These are teething problems in a new law. Majority of the companies that went through insolvency proceedings under IBC and ended in liquidation so far were already stressed entities for a long time whose value had been eroded significantly and were pending before the Board for Industrial and Financial Reconstruction (BIFR). The real impact of the IBC is to be seen in the fresh cases where I expect the law to provide an efficient avenue to effect a resolution.

The Reserve Bank circular dated June 7, 2019 has put in place a framework for resolution of stressed assets through which envisages a time bound implementation of a resolution plan, failing which disincentives in the form of additional provisions will not work.

These provisions are available for real sector firms; the situation is entirely different when it comes to resolution of financial firms. In this regard, the Government, on November 15, 2019 has notified the rules containing a framework for resolution of Financial Services Providers (FSPs) under the IBC. The applicability of these rules would be limited to certain financial services providers to be separately notified by the Government in consultation with regulators.

Resolute efforts towards recognition, repair and resolution have resulted in Non-Performing Assets (NPAs) of the banking system declining for the first time in March 2019 after a gap of 7 years. Fresh slippages declined and the system-level provision coverage ratio jumped to 60.5 percent from 48.3 percent a year ago. The capital adequacy ratio of the banking system has increased to 14.3 percent, much higher than the Basel norms. This has benefited from the recapitalisation of PSBs in the order of ₹ 2.9 lakh crore by the Government in the recent period.

Mergers of Public Sector Banks

The government, with an objective to create strong and competitive banks, has announced an amalgamation of PSBs in order to create stronger banks with global presence. This consolidation is in the direction of the recommendations of the first report of the Narasimham Committee in 1991, where the requirement for fewer but stronger banks for Indian economy had been highlighted. The idea was to enable such banks to compete at the national and international level. A well executed merger generates synergies of workforce and capital, helps in streamlining of operations and leads to significant improvements in efficiency. It can also entail diffusion of best practices across the board between banks. The bigger and agile banks, in principle, could reposition themselves with better branding exercises. The merger process has to be executed without creating any disruption in the normal functioning of these banks.

Non-Bank Financial Companies (NBFC) Sector

It is well recognised that NBFCs play a prominent role in the Indian financial system by catering to financial needs of a wide variety of customers and niche sectors, providing complementarity and competition to banks. The NBFC sector largely depends on market and bank borrowings, thereby creating a web of inter-linkages with banks and financial markets. As Housing Finance Companies (HFCs) now fall under the regulatory purview of the Reserve Bank, we are undertaking a review of extant regulations and are in the process of harmonising these regulations for HFCs with applicable regulations for NBFCs.

In the aftermath of the IL&FS crisis and subsequent defaults by a few companies, asset quality concerns have emerged, which imposes liquidity constraints on NBFCs. The Reserve Bank has been proactive in taking several measures to address these concerns and strengthen the regulatory and supervisory architecture of the NBFC sector, thereby ensuring that the sector remains stable and robust. RBI has attached considerable importance to make Financial Sector resilient through harmonization of regulations and a robust liquidity framework. RBI with guidelines on liquidity risk management framework for NBFCs. Objective is to ensure proper governance and risk management structures in NBFCs.

Urban Co-operative Banks

They contribute significantly in credit delivery and in bringing other financial services to the people. The performance of some of these institutions, however, has been hampered due to operational and governance issues. The recent unearthing of fraud in one of the Urban Co-operative Banks (UCBs) has brought up issues relating to their governance, prudent internal control mechanisms, and adequacy of checks and balances to the forefront.

The Urban Co-operative Banks were brought under the ambit of the Banking Regulation (BR) Act, 1949 with effect from March 1, 1966. Certain provisions of the BR Act, however, were not made applicable to them, limiting the scope of regulation and supervision over them[1]. Broadly speaking, banking-related functions of cooperative banks are regulated by the Reserve Bank and management-related functions are controlled by the concerned State/Central Government. The Reserve Bank's regulatory control over UCBs is affected due to this duality of control. RBI has made concerted efforts in the past to mitigate the adverse impact of dual regulation in the form of MoUs with State/ Central Governments and setting up of a State-level Task Force for Co-operative Urban Banks (TAFCUB). However, challenges still persist. At present, the Reserve Bank is working with the Government to amend the Act governing co-operative banks. We have suggested several legislative changes to the Central Government for better regulation and supervision of UCBs. On our part, we are reviewing the existing architecture of regulation and supervision of UCBs and shall carry out necessary changes in sync with the evolving requirements.

UCBs are likely to increasingly face competition from players such as Small Finance Banks (SFBs), Payments Banks, NBFCs and Micro-Finance Institutions (MFIs). It is, therefore, necessary for them to adopt robust technology to enable them to provide banking services at lower costs and with adequate safeguards. The Reserve Bank has been taking proactive steps to assist these institutions to adopt a robust IT infrastructure. The proposed national level Umbrella Organisation (UO) is expected to provide liquidity and capital support to member of co-operative banks, and will therefore contribute to the strength and vibrancy of the sector.

New Frontiers of Banking

The emergence of new banking models, in the form of Payments Banks and Small Finance Banks, have widened the horizons of banking in India. The Government and the Reserve Bank have taken several initiatives to encourage greater use of electronic payments[2] to achieve a 'less cash' society. These measures have led to digital payments[3] to GDP ratio rising to 8.6 percent at end-March 2019 from 6.7 percent at end-March 2016. During the same period, the number of per capita digital transactions rose from 4.6 to 17.6. Similarly, Fin-Tech is offering alternative models of lending and capital raising. In this regard, crowdfunding, peer-to-peer lending, invoice financing (Trade Receivables Discounting System (TReDs)) and digital lending have made their presence felt. They have helped in improving the efficiency of intermediation by bringing down the costs, sachetisation of products and services and in expanding the reach of financial services to a greater number of people.

Artificial Intelligence (AI), Machine Learning (ML) and Big Data are becoming central to financial services innovation. Analysis of vast amount of data, both structured and unstructured, has been made possible using these techniques. Increasing levels of expectations of compliance to regulations and a greater focus on data and reporting has brought RegTech and SupTech into limelight. They are being applied in areas such as risk management, regulatory reporting, data management, compliance, e-KYC/anti-money laundering (AML)/ Combating the Financing of Terrorism (CFT), and fraud prevention.

Conventional banking is making way for next-generation banking with focus on digitisation and modernisation. The need for brick and mortar branches is being reviewed continuously as digitisation has brought banking to the fingertips of the people, obviating the need to physically visit a bank branch. The transformation of the financial services landscape caused by technological innovations can blur the difference between a bank and a technology company, as technological giants are making rapid strides into areas such as payments, traditionally the domain of banks. This will present testing grounds for the regulators to delicately balance promotion of innovation and applying uniform supervisory and regulatory framework. Although India's debt-to-GDP ratio is deteriorating, many former central bankers have said that policymakers like RBI should not fear these rating agencies and be shackled by them. Irrespective of ratings the Indian Economy has retained the confidence of foreign investors, both in terms of foreign portfolio investment and foreign direct investment. As the macro-economic fundamentals of the Economy are sound.

Before any matter is referred to CBI or any other such agency or even before an investigation begins, the committee will go into it and see whether it's a business failure or a case of malfeasance. If the committee feels there is some wrongdoing, only then will the matter be referred to the investigative agencies.

If it's a case of business failure or a business decision that has gone wrong, and there is no malfeasance then adequate protection has been provided. This problem was there in the past. This mechanism set up by the government will help alleviate the situation a lot.

CBI Courts CVC Constrain Credit Decisions

Bankers fear of investigative agencies as that is coming in the way of bankers taking credit decisions and CVC has formed an advisory committee named Advisory Board for Banking and Financial Frauds. It's a five member committee. Before any matter is referred to CBI or any other such agency or even before an investigation begins, the committee will go into it and see whether it's a business failure or a case of malfeasance. If the committee feels there is some wrongdoing, only then will the matter be referred to the investigative agencies.

If it's a case of business failure or a business decision that has gone wrong, and there is no malfeasance then there is not much to fear for Banks.

JUDICIAL ACTIVISM: In the recent past several decisions of the RBI have been struck down by the courts as the banning of trade in Crypto Currency by the RBI this dents the position of the RBI as it is made to revoke its decisions and in some instances recall its circulars though in the crypto-currency case, while having an issue with the principle of proportionality, the Supreme Court has offered a palliative and observed that RBI is not just another regulator.

Concluding Observations

Those banks have a critical role in the economy. The privilege of raising unsecured liabilities from the society and generating revenue by deploying them in various avenues and ventures necessitates prudent risk assessment of such deployment. In this process, the banks do have a responsibility to shoulder when it comes to contributing to the growth of productive sectors of the economy including infrastructure.

Focusing on governance, risk management, internal audit and compliance functions in banks more closely. RBI needs to be ahead of the regulatory and supervisory curve to inspire confidence as an effective Supervisor recent Bank PMC, Yes Bank Failures and NBFC Failures, ILFS have considerably dented its halo. It must work hard to ensure necessary reforms to build a more resilient and robust banking system with the ability to support the economic trajectory and the rebound.

III. New Dimensions of Banking

Emerging Structure of Banking Post Covid-19 Pandemic

While global banking system will be in the process of addressing the gaps exposed by the financial crisis, consequent on the issues caused by the Pandemic. There is a near universal agreement on the impending global recession by all the practitioners of the dismal science. Perhaps traditional face to face banking will now be a thing of the past and reliance will be placed on algorithms and credit scoring techniques which will be refined as we go along the hump of years to come post the Pandemic. Numerous FinTech startups have formed, spanning the banking and financial services industry. They have entered the payments and remittance space in the sphere of peer-to-peer lending, crowd-funding, trade finance, insurance, account aggregation and wealth management. Through collaboration with FinTech players, several banks are applying a hybrid model where mobile services interact with banking services. These trends will increase with the millenials and in the Post Covid World.

Banks will be confronted with disintermediation from FinTech companies but also from large technology companies (BigTechs) which are entering into financial services industry in a big way. Building on the advantages of the reinforcing nature of their data network activities, some BigTechs are venturing into payments, money management, insurance and lending activities. At present financial services are only a small part of their business globally. But given their size and reach, their entry into financial services has the potential to bring about rapid transformation of the financial sector landscape. It may, of course, bring many potential benefits. Using big data, BigTechs can assess the riskiness of borrowers, reducing the need for collateral. Hence, their low-cost structure business can easily be scaled up to provide basic financial services to the unbanked population. Tech companies have disrupted retailing, media, transit and travel. Now the retail banking business model looks set to be transformed too.

These startups, they are laying siege to several areas of the banking industry. It shows that this assault is already well underway and that many incumbents are poised to be displaced, diminished and disintermediated. It draws on extensive research and on-and-off the record interviews with senior executives in some of the biggest banks.

Traditional banks need to reinvent themselves by launching a 'Beta Bank': a lean, stand-alone organisation fit for the future with an entirely new, contactless, and differentiated business model. Banks will become Brick and Mortar Dinosaurs banking regulators will have to reinvent themselves and up their game to stay relevant. Banks have to imbibe these new technology and business practices to remain competitive. Banking regulators, on the other hand, have to focus on achieving a balance between promoting innovation and applying a measured/ proportional supervisory and regulatory framework. All these mean that the future of banking will not be a continuam of the past. We would see a very different banking sector, in terms of structure and business model, in the Post Covid-19 Pandemic century.

Chapter - VI

Agriculture

The Agriculture sector contributes 16.5% of India's GDP and is a major source of livelihood for 60% of the population of 52% of the country's total labour force is directly engaged in agriculture or agricultural activities allied to Agriculture. It plays a significant role in the Indian economy and provides employment and livelihood to a large section of the Indian population. Agriculture has been characterised by weather dependence, fragmentation of land holdings production uncertainty and, colossal waste. These issues make agriculture risky and inefficient with respect to both input and output management. They need redress through higher productivity, cost effective production and higher monetisation of the produce to increase farmers income.

Declining Contribution to GDP

The contribution of agriculture to GDP has been declining from 52% in the 1950s to 30% in the 1990s and further below 20% from 2010 onwards as per data from Ministry of Statistics and Programme Implementation (MoSPI). In 2018-19, the share of Agriculture & Allied Gross Value Added (GVA) in overall GVA was 16% (Ministry of Agriculture and Farmers' Welfare (MoA&FW) Annual Report 2018-19). Economic Survey 2018-19 suggests that the growth rate in GVA (at 2011-12 prices) over past five-six years has been higher for livestocks, fishing and aquaculture as compared to crops allied activities contribute approximately 40% to agricultural output, whereas only 6-7% of agricultural credit flows towards allied activities.

Adverse Land Man Ratio

An important characteristic of Indian agriculture is that it is mainly small holders' farming with an average landholding size of 1.08 hectares.

The small and marginal farmers account for 86 percent of all holdings and 47 percent of the operated area. They contribute more than 50% of the total agricultural and allied output. In smallholder farming, it remains a challenge to raise agricultural productivity and farmers' incomes. It requires appropriate solutions starting with easy access to modern inputs and then selling the produce in most remunerative markets.

The Importance of Institutional Credit

Institutional credit at reasonable cost all along the value chain is one such catalytic instrument that can facilitate the process by converting many subsistence farmers into vibrant commercial farmers. They can then diversify their agricultural operations in growing high value crops like fruits and vegetables, and engage in allied activities, like dairy, poultry, fishery, honey, bee-keeping, etc. Allied has huge potential, which can be capitalised by improving credit flow towards it and by encouraging farmers to move towards allied activities.

Government Policy Prioritisation for Agriculture

The Government has introduced much needed structural reforms through three bills:

1. **The Farmers Produce Trade and Commerce (Promotion and Facilitation Ordinance 2020 better understood as getting away from the restrictive and malignant Agriculture Produce Marketing Act.**
2. "The Essential Commodities (Amendment) Ordinance, 2020" "The Freedom of Food Stocking by Agribusinesses Ordinance", and

3. "The Farmers (Empowerment and Protection) Agreement on Price Assurance and Farm Services Ordinance, 2020"as the Contract Farming Ordinance.
4. Free of the APMC the farmer will not be compelled to sell at the Mandis there will be better price discovery and he will earn more. This dispensation enables the farmer the freedom to transact with companies which may offer a better deal this allows for greater facility and agency. From farm gate to food plate becomes a reality.
5. The Agri Budget has been substantially increased the Swaminathan Committee had recommended the payment of MSP at 50% profits on the cost of production.
6. Establishing e-Nam, Electronic National Agriculture Markets.
7. An Agriculture Infrastructure fund under Atma Nirbhar Bharat Package.
8. The setting up and encouragement of Farmer Producer Organisations.
9. The farmers will have unobstructed interstate and intrastate Trade, outside the APMC and State controlled Mandis the removal of the Mandi Tax will lead to a single agricultural market.
10. Adoption of quality and grading standards will be enabled ensuring remunerative prices to the farmer.
11. Linkage of farming agreements with Insurance and Credit Instruments allowing transfer of the risk of market unpredictability from the farmer to the sponsor.
12. Enable farmer access to best in class technology and inputs as per contract farming with corporate.

the evolution of aggregate supply conditions in 2019-20, agriculture and allied activities provided a silver lining, with record food grains and horticulture production and favourable terms of trade for the farm economy. The challenge of managing supply gluts in cereals exposed the shortcomings of policy interventions in the form of price support and buffer stocking. Paradoxically, disruptions in agricultural supply chains and restrictions affecting transportation of agri-produce from farms to markets produced demand-supply mismatches that fuelled price flares in the second half of the year. The recent spate of reforms to agricultural marketing and infrastructure could open up new opportunities for agriculture if they could be complemented by trade policies that are predictable, expose the farm sector to international terms of trade and shift emphasis to processing and value addition. Shifting the terms of trade in favour of agriculture is the key to sustaining this dynamic change and generating positive supply responses in agricultural production. Experience shows that in periods when the terms of trade remained favourable to agriculture, annual average growth in agricultural gross value added (GVA) exceeded 3 percent. Hitherto, the main instrument of incentive has been minimum support prices, but the experience has been that price incentives have been costly, inefficient and even distortive. India has now reached a stage in which surplus management has become a major challenge. The priority is to move to policy strategies that ensure a sustained increase in farmers' income alongside reasonable food prices for consumers. An efficient domestic supply chain becomes critical here. Accordingly, the focus must now turn to the major reforms that are underway to facilitate free trade in agriculture. First, the amendment of the Essential Commodities Act (ECA) is intended to encourage private investment in supply chain infrastructure, including warehouses, cold storages and marketplaces. Second, the Farmers' Produce Trade and Commerce (Promotion and Facilitation) Ordinance, 2020 is aimed at facilitating barrier-free trade in agriculture produce. Third, the Farmers (Empowerment and Protection) Agreement on Price Assurance and Farm Services Ordinance, 2020 will empower farmers to engage with processors, aggregators, wholesalers, large retailers, and exporters in an effective and transparent manner. With this enabling legislative framework, the focus must turn to (a) crop diversification, de-emphasising water guzzlers, however difficult it may be; (b) food processing that enhances shelf life of farm produce and minimises post-harvest wastes; (c) agricultural exports which expose the Indian farmer to international terms of trade and technology; and (d) public and private capital formation in the farm sector. (RBI Annual Report, 2020)

Indian agriculture sector is a net exporter of several commodities like rice, marine products, cotton, etc. Some of the important initiatives taken by the Government include the implementation of Interest Subvention Scheme (ISS) for providing credit for crop production at reduced interest rate, Soil Health Cards (SHC) for improving agricultural productivity, Pradhan Mantri Krishi Sinchai Yojana (PMKSY) to ensure irrigation facilities, Pradhan Mantri Fasal Bima Yojana (PMFBY), for providing a safety net against natural calamities and National Agriculture Market Scheme (e-NAM) for providing better price discovery through transparent auction process. There is also a renewed focus on allied activities to aid income of farmers. Despite these initiatives, there are several challenges confronting Indian agriculture.

Challenges

1. Diminishing and degrading natural resources,
2. Fragmented land holdings fragmented land holdings Land fragmentation due to adverse land/man ratio,
3. Rapidly increasing demand for food (not just for quantity but also for quality,
4. Stagnating farm incomes, and
5. Unprecedented climate change,
6. These need to be tackled for long term sustainability and viability of Indian agriculture.

Role of Institutional Credit in Indian Agriculture

Banks in India have made commendable progress in terms of scale and outreach of formal credit to the agriculture sector. From ₹ 31.71 billion in 1981, the outstanding advances to agriculture and allied activities have grown significantly to ₹ 13694.56 billion in 2017-18 (16 percent of total bank credit). The long-term trend in institutional agricultural credit revealed that over time, significant progress has been achieved in terms of scale.

Agricultural credit as a percentage to Agriculture GDP increased from 10% in 1970s to 52% by 2018, which shows that banks have made significant progress in lending to agriculture. In India, scheduled

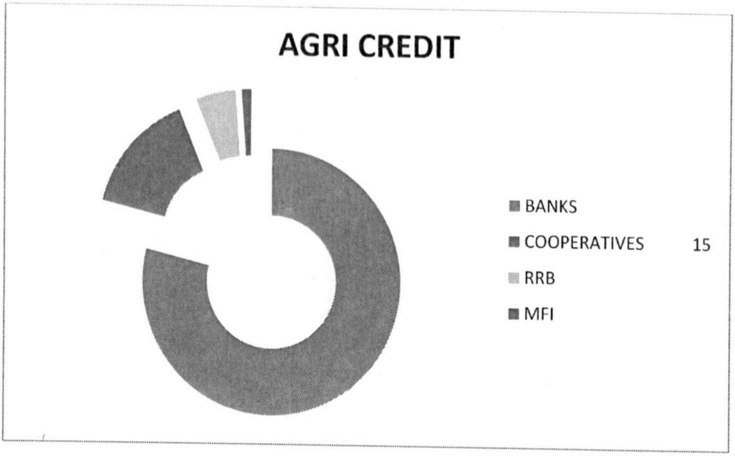

commercial banks (79%) are the major players in supplying credit to agriculture sector followed by rural cooperative banks (15%), regional rural banks (5%) and micro finance institutions (1%). Small finance banks set up with the objective of deepening financial inclusion have started their operations recently. It is expected that they would meet the needs of small farmers they would be catering to small and marginal farmers, low income households, small businesses and other unorganised entities.

Challenges in Agriculture Financing

Despite the impressive growth in formal agricultural credit, there are still several challenges that need to be tackled. Data on the average loan taken by agricultural households, as per the NABARD's Financial Inclusion Survey Report 2016-17, indicated that 72% of the credit requirement was met from institutional sources and 28% from noninstitutional sources.

The report further states that out of the total agricultural households, approximately 30 percent still avail credit from noninstitutional sources. The problem of financial exclusion gets aggravated due to lack of legal framework for landless cultivators as the absence of documentary evidence becomes a major hindrance for extending credit to this segment of the farming community, who take up cultivation work on oral lease. Further, the analysis of state-wise flow of institutional agricultural credit has revealed uneven distribution of credit amongst states compared to their corresponding share in overall output. To a certain extent, such regional disparity is on account of variation in credit absorption capacity of these regions. Funds like Rural Infrastructure Development Fund (RIDF) have been created out of priority sector lending shortfall of banks and established with NABARD with the underlying philosophy of lending to state governments to facilitate creation of enabling rural infrastructure to deepen the credit absorption capacity in rural areas.

Rural Infrastructure Development Fund

An analysis of sanctions from RIDF indicates that states with higher credit flow made higher demands for resources under the fund. On the contrary, states with lower credit flow were lagging in borrowing funds from RIDF. Thus, the least developed states which are already credit starved are getting lower share of funds from the RIDF. This highlights the need to break this vicious cycle and think of certain measures by which funds can be earmarked to the most backward/ credit starved regions to ensure speedier development of the most backward areas in the country. We may also have to think of ways to incentivise banks to lend in these backward areas so that both demand and supply side issues are addressed. These issues and challenges impinge on the efficiency, inclusiveness and sustainability of the agricultural credit system, which is a matter of concern.

RBI Internal Working Group

RBI had set up an Internal Working Group (IWG) in February 2019, to understand the issues and recommend workable solutions to address the constraints. The IWG based on in-depth data analysis and research held extensive consultations and deliberations with experts and practitioners in the field and submitted its report in September 2019.

The policy interventions recommended by the IWG include

1. Building up of an enabling ecosystem,
2. Digitisation of land records,
3. Reforming land lease framework,

4. Creation of a National level agency to build consensus among the state governments and central government with regard to agriculture-related policy reforms:
    - Innovative digital solutions to bridge the information gap between the banks and farmers for expediting the credit delivery process.
    - Further changes in the Priority Sector Lending guidelines applicable to all banks.
    - Strengthening of credit delivery channels through Kisan Credit Cards, Self-Help Group Bank Linkage Programme, Farmer Producers Organisations, in a manner to make them more effective and efficient in ensuring credit flow to the credit starved regions of the country, as also to the excluded segments of the farming community.
    - If implemented effectively these would go a long way in ensuring the long-term sustainability and viability of the Indian agriculture sector.

Agriculture is important from two standpoints:

1. The first is FOOD SECURITY, which is predicated on adequate supply of food for humans and, feed and fibre for livestock.
2. Secondly, Inflation control

    The Indian economy today needs both low and stable inflation as well as boost to spending, which is best guaranteed by increased farm production and incomes.

The brewing issues in the villages as a result of the onslaught of the Covid Pandemic:

- Because of significant disruption in supply chains as a result of the lockdown, farmers are stuck with a large amount of produce, especially of perishables like milk, fruits and vegetables, flowers and even poultry meat and eggs.
- Due to this glut, farm prices are collapsing, pushing farmers into destitution. Many of them are dumping milk and vegetables on the roads.

- With the procurement season for rabi crops having started, the mandi system will choke, if immediate steps are not taken to organise procurement operations in an orderly manner.

Steps being taken by the Department of Agriculture Cooperation and Farmers' Welfare for smooth harvesting of Rabi Crop and sowing of summer crop

A lot of rabi crop has already been harvested, but for the crop still standing, there could be shortage of farm labour, as a panicked exodus of migrant workers explodes around us. After the crop is harvested, it has to be packed and transported to markets, which again needs workers, vehicle drivers, and uninterrupted movement.

- Video conference was conducted with all States and Insurance companies to review the payment of claims, status of Conduct of CCEs for Rabi 2019-20 crops, crop loss survey and implementation of Smart Sampling Technique.
- For facilitating farm insurance, letters issued to all States to issue passes to representatives of concerned Insurance companies for co-witnessing Crop Cutting Experiments and to relax the norms for conducting field level survey for intimation received for Post-Harvest crop losses due to unseasonal rainfall and hailstorm.
- Phytosanitary certification for export consignments and Import releases of plant and plant products are continuing.
- Enabling FPOs to upload produce from collection centers with picture/quality parameter and also avail bidding facility without going to mandis, which will reduce their logistic costs and hassle to sell their produce.
- e-NAM platform has created an interface with large transport aggregators like Blackbuck, Rivigo, Mavyn, Truck Suvidha, Truck Guru, Transin Logistics, Elastic Run etc. This would help traders to find and arrange timely movement of produces from mandi to various other locations.
- e-NAM platform/ mobile app has been further strengthened with 'Farmers friendly' features such as advance registration

of the lot through app which in turn will reduce waiting time for farmers at gate entry of the mandi and will bring huge efficiency and will facilitate smooth arrival recording at gate.

- For providing support to horticulture crops necessary coordination is being done with growers, aggregators, wholesalers, mandi associations, State Horticulture Missions, for smooth transport of the commodities and to sort out all difficulties.
- Lockdown Outreach
- In lockdown period, Kisan Call Centres at all 21 locations are being operated by diverting calls to individual mobile numbers of Farm Tele Advisors, who are now operating from homes.
- Shops of Agricultural machinery, its spare parts (including its supply chain) & repairs and shops for truck repairs on highways, preferably at fuel pumps, can remain open in order to facilitate transportation of farm produce.
- Besides, tea industry, including plantations can function with maximum of 50% workers.

Further Solutions

Agri-Marketing Reforms

- Abolish/reframe the APMC Act and encourage direct buying of agri-produce from farmers/Farmer Producer Organisations (FPOs).
- Warehouses can also be designated as markets, and the warehouse receipt system can be scaled up.
- The private sector should be encouraged to open mandis with modern infrastructure, capping commissions.
- Futures trading should be encouraged by allowing banking finance to hedge for commodity price risks.
- Procurement must be staggered through coupons and incentives that give farmers an additional bonus for bringing produce to the market after May 10, or so.

- The APMC mandis can be better structured, with smaller mandis allowed to be set up in government schools or other areas instead of people converging at one big market. Farmers can be given day-wise or hour-wise slots, along with clear assurances that the sale of their produce will be looked-after.

Under e-NAM: Promote e-NAM through proper assaying and grading the produce and setting up dispute settlement mechanism; rope in major logistics players for delivery of goods.

PM Kisan: The amount provided under PM Kisan should be increased from ₹ 6,000 to at least ₹ 10,000 per farming family to partially compensate them for their losses.

Fundamental reforms in the UN System: India must ask for fundamental reforms in the UN System, including the WHO, making it more transparent, competent, and accountable.

Policy Focus: This sector of the economy should become a priority again in term of policies.

More Investments: Indian agriculture needs more investments (in irrigation, for instance) and more financial support (by strengthening the MGNREGA, among other things). But not only that.

The issue of Liberalisation: Further liberalisation of Indian agriculture would hamper food security as the existing food procurement system is essential in maintaining food reserves and protection of vulnerable farmers from the whims of the global markets with the minimum support price offered for wheat and rice under the Agricultural Produce Market Committee (APMC) Act.

Introduction of agro-ecological system of farming: The transition to an agro-ecological system of agriculture has the capacity to become the engine to restart a sustainable economy by increasing soil fertility and reducing ground water exploitation.

- An agro-ecological transition will regenerate not only the soil which was depleted due to the excessive use of chemical pesticides but also ensure sustainable supply of food in the long run.

- It will make the system more resilient overall and provide a safety net for farmers in case of crop damage due to factors such as climate change or droughts.
- It will also strengthen food security and help the nation fight hunger and malnutrition.

It will help bridge the urban-rural divide as much-needed investment will occur in rural areas after decades of neglect that created the staggering inequalities. Farmers have completed sowing of kharif crops in nearly 55 percent of the season's normal area by the first week of July. Last year at this time, they had achieved hardly 38 percent coverage, while undertaking the bulk of plantings after mid-July and all through August. The primary reason has been the southwest monsoon's timely onset and the country receiving 14 percent above normal rains so far. With water levels in major reservoirs at 146 percent of the last 10-years' average for this time and groundwater tables recharged from the good pre-monsoon showers as well, farmers have sought to capitalise on the excellent soil moisture conditions. Not surprisingly, every crop — from paddy and pulses to maize, bajra, jowar, small millets, soyabean, sesamum, groundnut and cotton — has posted a significant acreage jump over last kharif. Fertiliser sales registering high double-digit growth every month from November is further proof of farmers' inclination to plant and also invest in their crop.

Simply put, India is headed for a bumper kharif harvest on top of the recent rabi or winter-spring crop. This is, of course, subject to the monsoon not playing truant in the second half (August-September) and also no locust attacks. Last year, there was very little rainfall till the last week of July, after which it poured so much that 2019 ended up as the wettest year in a quarter of a century. The opposite happening — good rains now giving way to extended dry spells — cannot be ruled out this year. One needs to equally watch out for locust swarms: The Food and Agricultural Organisation has warned about breeding already occurring along the Indo-Pakistan border. These could lead to "substantial hatching and band formation" this month and cause the first-generation of inbred swarms to form by mid-August. That is when the kharif crop, too, would be in the vegetative growth stage. Government agencies need to be on high alert during the next 4-5 weeks and take pre-emptive control measures, including aerial spraying operations in the main scheduled desert breeding areas.

- Farmers have completed sowing of kharif crops in nearly 55 percent of the season's normal area by the first week of July. Last year at this time, they had achieved hardly 38 percent coverage, while undertaking the bulk of plantings after mid-July and all through August. The primary reason has been the southwest monsoon's timely onset and the country receiving 14 percent above-normal rains so far. With water levels in major reservoirs at 146 percent of the last 10-years' average for this time and groundwater tables recharged from the good pre-monsoon showers as well, farmers have sought to capitalise on the excellent soil moisture conditions. Not surprisingly, every crop — from paddy and pulses to maize, bajra, jowar, small millets, soyabean, sesamum, groundnut and cotton — has posted a significant acreage jump over last kharif. Fertiliser sales registering high double-digit growth every month from November is further proof of farmers' inclination to plant and also invest in their crop.
- As things stand, agriculture is one sector that seems to hold out hope, even as manufacturing, retail and other services continue to grapple with uncertainty from rising COVID cases and localised lockdowns. The Narendra Modi government did well to ensure smooth harvesting of the rabi crop and also minimum support price-based procurement in respect of wheat, paddy, chana, rapeseed-mustard and tur. No major reports have come of shortage of fertiliser, seed and other inputs for the current kharif season either. The recent reforms involving removal of stockholding limits on foodstuffs and allowing farm produce to be traded outside regulated mandis may not have any substantial immediate impact. But they send out the right signals about a sector whose growth, employment and value creation potential, both on- and off-farm, hasn't really been realised.

Chapter - VII

Digital India and Financial Inclusion

> *"Universal access to financial services is within reach—thanks to new technologies, transformative business models and ambitious reforms... As early as 2020, such instruments as e-money accounts, along with debit cards and low-cost regular bank accounts, can significantly increase financial access for those who are now excluded."*
>
> — **Jim Yong Kim**
>
> President, World Bank Group

Digital Financial Inclusion

With the prospect of reaching billions of new customers, banks and nonbanks have begun to offer digital financial services for financially excluded and underserved populations, building on the approaches that have been used for years to improve access channels for those already served by banks and other financial institutions.

Financial Innovation- Innovative digital financial services involving the use of mobile phones have been launched in more than 80 countries (GSMA 2014). As a result of the significant advances in the accessibility and affordability provided by digital financial services, millions of poor customers are moving from exclusively cash-based transactions to formal financial services. The benefits of this development include economic growth and stability, both for the customers and for the economies where they and their families reside.

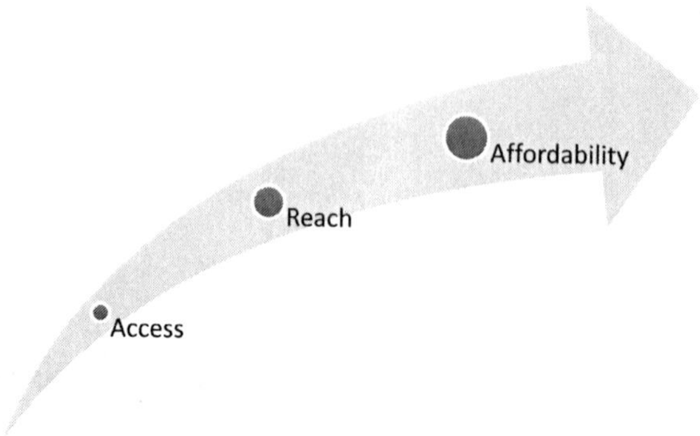

The Power of the Mobile Phone — "Everybody Has One"

India has a high penetration of mobile phones there are 12 million users of Phones in India and 31.7% of India's population used a mobile phone in 2020.

However, the use of digital financial services by formerly excluded customers brings not only benefits but also risks, due in part to the characteristics of a typical poor customer (inexperienced with formal financial services and unfamiliar with consumer rights). Some of the risks are new while others, although well known, may take on different dimensions in the financial inclusion context.

This book aims to provide national and global policy-makers with a clear picture of the rapid march of digital financial services for the poor and the need for their attention and informed understanding. It proposes a concise definition of "digital financial inclusion" and summarizes its impact on financially excluded and underserved populations; outlines the new and shifting risks of digital financial inclusion models that are significant to regulators, supervisors, and standard-setting bodies (SSBs); and concludes with observations on digital financial inclusion issues on the policy-making horizon.

Definition

"Digital financial inclusion" can be defined as digital access to and use of formal financial services by excluded and underserved populations. Such services should be suited to the customers' needs and delivered responsibly, at a cost both affordable to customers and sustainable for providers.

Providers

Today's providers of such financial services can be divided into four broad groupings based on the party holding the contractual relationship with the customer: (i) a full-service bank offering a "basic" or "simplified" transactional account for payments, transfers, and value storage via mobile device or payment card plus point-of-sale (POS) terminal; (ii) a limited-service niche bank offering such an account via mobile device or payment card plus POS terminal; (iii) a mobile network operator (MNO) e-money issuer; and (iv) a nonbank non-MNO e-money issuer. All four models function via three components: a digital transactional platform, an agent network, and the customer's access device. With these components in place, payments and transfers, as well as credit, savings, insurance, and even securities, can be offered digitally to excluded and underserved customers.

Jan Dhan–Aadhaar–Mobile (JAM) trinity has a positive impact on the banking sector and financial inclusion in the country. Jan Dhan accounts are no-frills accounts which can be opened with ease. These accounts are linked to Aadhaar numbers of the individuals, which in turn is linked to the Direct Benefit Transfer (DBT) scheme. With the launch of JAM services, there has been a significant improvement in terms of targeted and accurate payments. They have also helped in weeding out duplication of entries, and bringing down the reliance on cash mode of payments.

Financial inclusion is the cornerstones of the Indian economy. Digital India is a substantive intervention to bring the unbanked, relegated to the margins of the mainstream economy, into the formal financial economy as producers and consumers of goods and services. While there has been an increase in digital transactions across the country, issues the ability of formal financial sector institutions to secure last-mile connectivity, high costs of administration of services, high dormancy of accounts are being recognized and slowly addressed.

Financial inclusion is mainstreaming the marginalized, through financial literacy and access to banking and financial services. It is a multidimensional approach that involves bringing on board various stakeholders from the government and the people. Digital India initiatives under Digital India, like easy banking facilities for all, simplification of procedures relating to financial instruments like Permanent Account Number (PAN), unique identification process of Aadhaar, simplification of tax procedures through the goods and services tax (GST), etc. have contributed significantly to the efforts of financial inclusion in the country.

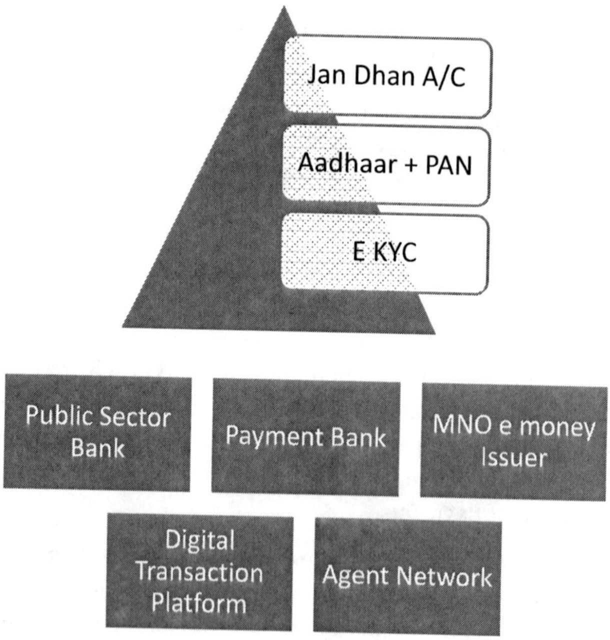

This chapter analyses the impact of such initiatives, and the scope of Digital India in converting traditional manual procedures of availing government services into electronic ones. Besides, the impact of Digital India on important sectors, such as direct and indirect taxation structures, banking institutions, and delivery of government schemes.

Global Findex Report

The efficacy of Digital India vis-à-vis financial inclusion can be measured by the growth in digital transactions and the proportion of the poor and their ability to access banking facilities. According to the World Bank's Global Financial Inclusion Database or Global Findex report (2017), 80% Indian adults have a bank account—27 points higher than the 53% estimated in the Findex 2014 round. The Findex 2017 report also estimates that 77% Indian women have bank accounts, against 43% and 26% respectively in 2014 and 2011 (Qazi, 2019). These figures, however, contrast with the statistics from the other spectrum. According to the same report, about 190 million adults in India do not have a bank account, making India the world's second largest nation in terms of unbanked population after China (World Bank, 2017b).

Digital Ecosystem

The concept of financial inclusion has evolved over a period, and has been studied by policymakers and researchers. India has developed its financial ecosystem and has brought about major changes to increase the last-mile connectivity of financial services. The intent has been to provide the underprivileged and marginalized access to financial resources to improve their lives. It has been observed that financial inclusion has the potential to reduce poverty, create jobs, improve opportunities, health and education.

The lack of inclusive growth, due to large inequalities in economic and/or social realms, often translate into inequalities in terms of opportunities, leading to huge disparities in the critical sectors of health and education (Goldberg, 2019). Traditionally, institutions like the Reserve Bank of India (RBI) and National Bank for Agriculture and Rural Development (NABARD) have pioneered initiatives to promote financial inclusion.

1. The opening of bank branches in remote areas, the post-nationalization push of the Banking System to improve its reach and spread.
2. Issuing Kisan Credit Cards (KCC).
3. JAM: Jan Dhan-Adhaar Mobile thereby Leveraging information technology to spread awareness and literacy.
4. Linkage of self-help groups (SHGs) with banks.
5. Innovating Micro ATMs and increasing the number of automated teller machines (ATMs).
6. Introducing the business correspondents, extending the reach of the formal banking system.
7. Innovating new financial products.
8. Increasing credit facilities and
9. Increasing insurance covers (life, health, livestock for the marginalised.

RBI Data

As per RBI data, RBI, Kerala, Maharashtra, and Karnataka have achieved high financial inclusion (Index on Financial Inclusion (IFI) > 0.5), while Tamil Nadu, Punjab, Andhra Pradesh, Himachal Pradesh, Sikkim, and Haryana have been identified as a cohort of medium financial inclusion (0.3–0.5). The remaining states have been categorised as states with low financial inclusion states (< 0.3). These figures are important, because they indicate three critical variables of financial inclusion, namely penetration of financial services (number of adults having bank accounts), availability of banking services (number of bank branches per population of 1,000), and the usage of the financial services (measured as outstanding credit and deposit).

BASIC BANK ACCOUNTS, the objective is to provide no-frills bank accounts to every individual above 10 years of age across the country, even in the remotest parts. As per the estimates in March 2020, the total number of accounts are more than 380 million (Ministry of Finance, 2020). The introduction of unique identification Aadhaar number has also contributed to the financial inclusion in the country. By significantly changing the concept of individual identity, Aadhaar has not only brought about a secure and easily verifiable system but also easy to obtain as well to help in the financial inclusion process. The combination of Aadhaar, PMJDY, and a surge in mobile communication has reshaped the way citizens access government services.

Digital India and the Reliance on Technology

The concept of Digital India is driven by the idea that a large country like India cannot place reliance only on traditional public service delivery mechanisms. With limited resources and a huge population to cater to the use of technology has been ramped up in order to provide government facilities to maximum numbers of people, and, in the process, ensure transparency and accountability.

The expectations of citizens from government include

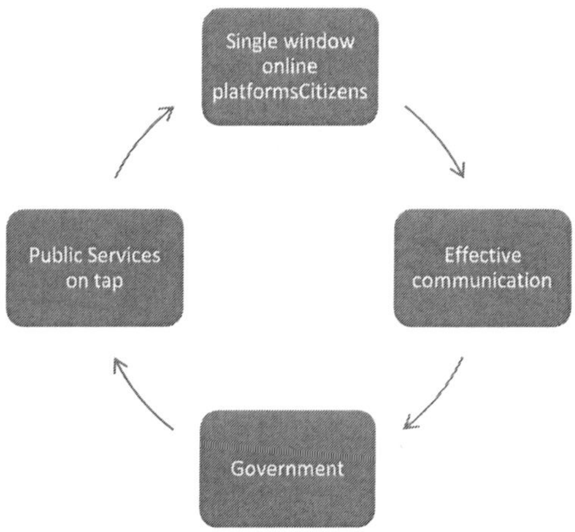

on-demand availability of public services, single-window online platforms, one-point help centres, and effective communication and alerts. Digital India aims to meet these expectations by building electronic portals for service delivery, creating necessary support infrastructure, integrating government services and databases, and enhancing the skills of the stakeholders through awareness programmes and trainings.

Proliferation of Payment Facilities

The launch of Digital India has brought about a change in terms of payment facilities available to the stakeholders, from the underprivileged sections. KCC, general credit cards (GCC), and mobile banking facilities have been encouraging the poor to participate in the digital ecosystem. With the strengthening of the Unified Payment Interface (UPI) by RBI, digital payments have seen increased adoption. To this end, many payment gateways have come up to further improve digital transfers.

Increase in Volume of Digital Transactions

As per a World Bank report, the total volume of digital transactions in India

1. Net banking,
2. Mobile banking,
3. Debit cards,
4. Credit cards,
5. Prepaid instruments,
6. Mobile wallets.

Showed compound annual growth rate (CAGR) of 30% from 1,142 million in April 2015 to 1,928 million in April 2017. On the other hand, mobile banking transactions grew more than five times, from 19.75 million in April 2015 to 106.18 million in April 2017. Similarly, mobile wallet transactions grew from 11.96 million transactions in April 2015 to 387.6 million transactions worth ₹ 15,408 crore in January 2020 (World Bank 2018; RBI 2020).

A valid bank account and mobile phone can facilitate quicker and easier payments. The payment system has been made more accessible due to offline transaction-enabling platforms, like Unstructured Supplementary Service Data (USSD), which makes it possible to use mobile banking services without internet, even on a basic mobile handset. On the other hand, the Aadhar-enabled payment system (AEPS) enables an Aadhar enabled bank account (AEBA) to be used at any place and at any time, using micro ATMs.

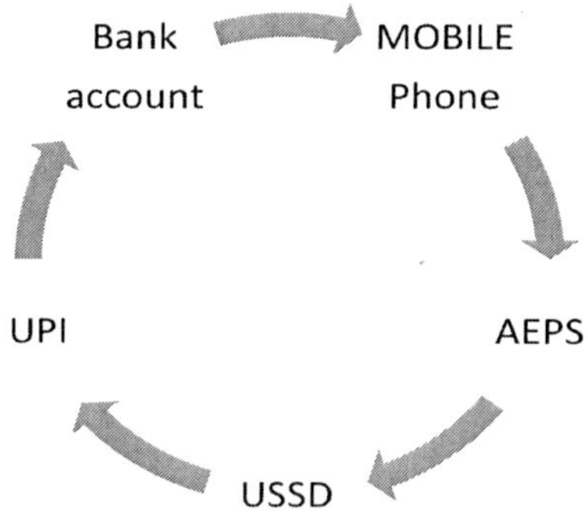

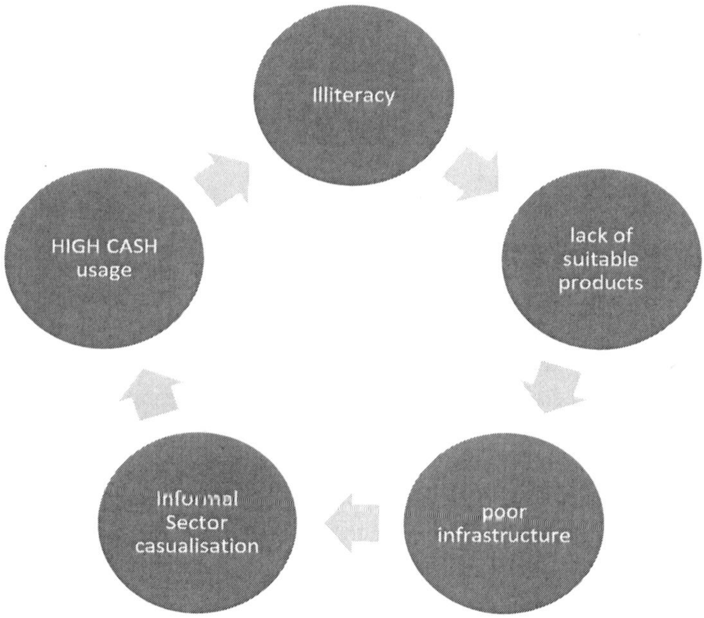

E-governance Platforms

There have been efforts to increase the scope of Digital India to align with the working of multiple departments and government schemes, in meeting the objective of financial inclusion.

Income Tax department, due to the introduction of e-governance platforms. The key services, like income tax returns (ITR) filing, tax deducted at source (TDS) compliance, and refund delivery mechanism, have been made online.

Out of the 66.8 million ITRs filed in the financial year 2018–19, 65 million ITRs (98%) were filed electronically, and 95% of the refunds were electronically remitted to the taxpayers (Income Tax Department, 2019). So, one does not have to run from pillar to post for a refund. On the compliance front, 1.5 million notices/letters were issued electronically in fiscal 2017–18, and 89% of all notices and letters were delivered through e-mails (Income Tax Department 2018). All these initiatives have proved to be significant as they ensure that financial inclusion expands to other institutions, and not just confined to the banking sector.

Bottlenecks and Major Challenges

There is no doubt that India has significantly improved the financial inclusion of the marginalised sections, and Digital India has turned out to be an important intervention. However, the digital divide is too wide and there exist many bottlenecks and challenges which need immediate attention.

To begin with, High Level Principles for Digital Financial Inclusion, published by the G 20 under the rubric of Global Partnership for Financial Inclusion in 2016, provides useful insights to address the issues impeding financial inclusion, and how digital technologies can help in the process (World Bank, 2017b). These include the promotion of financial services as a national plan, the need to balance innovation and risk, providing legal and regulatory frameworks, and expanding the digital financial ecosystems, among others. Similarly, it suggests the need to ramp up investments for digital tools that can help integrate systems and databases making it easier for auditors and regulators to process information. It also highlights that the advent of digital systems would mean huge data volumes and without the presence of adequate data mining and data analytics, countries would have to handle too much data with limited outcomes.

The most common barriers to the digital financial inclusion include the non-availability of suitable financial products, lack of skills among the stakeholders to use digital services, infrastructural issues, teething problems between various systems, and low-income consumers who are not able to afford the technology required to get onto the digital platform.

Another challenge to digital financial inclusion arises from the attitude of the stakeholders. For instance, take the case of Jan Dhan bank accounts. As with all government schemes, banks were given ambitious targets to open accounts for the marginalised. This has resulted in the opening of many dormant accounts which never saw actual banking transactions. All such activities lead to high costs for Banks, with poor returns and thus, huge operative costs only proved to be detrimental to the actual objective.

Casualisation of Employment

Another major bottleneck faced by Digital India, with respect to financial inclusion, is the heavily dominated cash economy in the country. The data from RBI reveals that cash circulation has increased in 2018 after demonetisation. As per a report of the International Labour Organization (ILO), about 81% of the employed persons in India work in the informal sector (ILO 2018). The combination of a huge informal sector along with a high dependence on cash mode of transaction poses an impediment to digital financial inclusion.

Gender and Exclusion

There is also a gender dimension to financial inclusion in the country. According to the 2017 Global Findex database, 83% of males above 15 years of age in India held accounts at a financial institution in 2017 compared to 77% females (World Bank, 2018). This is attributed to socio-economic factors, including the availability of mobile handset and internet data facility being higher among men than women.

In conclusion, for the success of digital initiatives, there has to be a multidimensional approach through which existing digital platforms, infrastructure, human resources, and policy frameworks are strengthened (Kim, 2014). More importantly, human resources should be leveraged by skilling and positively engaging with them to achieve the last-mile connectivity of financial institutions.

If corrective measures are taken to tide over the existing problems, interventions, such as Digital India, have the potential to amplify the benefits of economic growth to the poor. Not only will it reduce the costs for the financial institutions, but it would also address safety concerns and accuracy of the data involved in financial transactions.

As the country move towards a cashless economy, it is vital that financial institutions invest in a secure digital payments ecosystem that promotes financial inclusion, is transparent and easy to use.

In recent years, the digital payments ecosystem in India has come of age. An increased number of consumers in the country are now choosing to make digital payments for their purchases. This growth is being driven by segments such as mobile wallets and buy now pay later (BNPL).

According to KPMG, digital payments in the country are growing at a CAGR of 12.7%. This is a highly significant figure which indicates the rapid growth of the industry.

As India moves towards its goal of becoming a cashless economy, it is extremely important for us to understand the importance of secure digital payments. This article discusses the key methods being used to build a secure digital payments ecosystem and highlights why these payments are imperative in today's connected world.

Combating the threats to digital payments

While the digital payments industry continues to grow rapidly, there are numerous threats that could hamper its adoption in the country. Some of these threats include hacking, cyber fraud, malware, and ransomware.

These threats can arise from both the merchant side as well as the buyer side. During 2018-19 alone, India recorded 1,477 instances of digital fraud. Therefore, all stakeholders must work in unison in order to negate these threats and ensure that digital payments work in a seamless manner.

Several steps have already been taken in this regard. For instance, leading fintech companies are already investing significant sums of money in order to safeguard their digital payments infrastructure. Some of the technologies that are helping these organisations in securing their transactions include 3D secure protocols, two-factor authorisation, as well as highly secure networks.

In addition to this, financial institutions in the country are also protecting their payment mechanisms by building robust cybersecurity teams. Leading banks are resorting to hiring cybersecurity professionals such as ethical hackers in order to test the strength of their payment systems. Similarly, payment processing firms are also strengthening their resources against online fraud by resorting to risk detection techniques.

The growing importance of secure digital payments

Over the past couple of years, secure digital payments have emerged as a critical component of our lives. This is because of the numerous benefits that this form of payment provides. Some of these benefits are highlighted below.

1. **Promoting financial inclusion**

   Firstly, digital payments have become a major tool to promote financial inclusion in the country. In a densely-populated nation like India, it is not possible for banks to be omnipresent and cater to the needs of all the people. This is where digital payments can prove to be a great way to provide financial services to the far-flung.

   Further, the digital payments ecosystem must be completely secure because most of the marginalised communities cannot afford instances of fraud. If implemented in the right way, secure digital payments can transform the way rural India operates.

2. **Transparency and accountability**

   Secondly, secure digital payments also ensure a greater degree of transparency and accountability. Although cash has been used for centuries, there is little transparency in its usage. Further, it can be a complex task to keep track of your cash transactions, leaving you vulnerable against pilferages and thefts.

On the other hand, secure digital payments ensure that all your transactions can easily be traced. Similarly, secure gateways are harder to tamper with, thereby providing an extra layer of security.

3. **Convenience and ease of use**

   Nowadays, most people do not have the time or energy to wait for their payment transactions to be executed. Instead, they want immediate payment solutions and quick confirmation messages. The advent of secure digital payments has meant that both these needs are being met. Modern-day digital payments have become so efficient that they are completed within a matter of seconds. Further, digital payment transactions are highly secure, which ensures that consumers can attain peace of mind.

4. **Reduced transaction costs**

   Digital payment systems that are highly secure can also help all stakeholders in reducing transaction costs. This happens because these systems are protected against unauthorised access. As these systems continue to evolve and become more efficient, the transaction costs are likely to come down even further. This could prove to be a major benefit for the consumers and merchants, who can seamlessly access funds without having to worry about external threats.

Conclusion

To sum up, it is evident that secure digital transactions are a given in today's world.

The benefits of secure digital payments far outweigh any risks, thereby driving their growth. In the near future, it is likely that digital payments will become even more secure as fintech providers start to leverage advanced technologies such as machine learning and natural language processing.

These technologies will further increase the importance of secure digital payments, making them an inseparable part of our lives.

Globally, financial sector policymakers recognize the "game-changing" potential of digital financial inclusion. At an October 2014 conference, Jamie Caruana, General Manager of the Bank for International Settlements, emphasized this point by noting that institutions including the G 20 and global financial regulators "have the opportunity - and indeed the responsibility - to prepare the standard-setting world for both the risks and the rewards of the digitization of financial services."

What, exactly, did Mr. Caruana mean by "digital financial inclusion" and why does it matter, both to this audience of global policy leaders and to the estimated 2.5 billion mostly poor and low-income adults who today transact mostly or entirely in cash? To which risks and which rewards is he referring – and who stands to gain or lose? A new CGAP Brief distills answers to these and related questions.

Defining the key components of "digital financial inclusion"

"Digital financial inclusion" can be defined broadly as digital access to and use of formal financial services by excluded and underserved populations. Such services should be suited to customers' needs, and delivered responsibly, at a cost both affordable to customers and sustainable for providers. There are three key components of any such digital financial services: a **digital transactional platform, retail agents**, and the use by customers and agents of a **device** – most commonly a mobile phone – to transact via the platform.

- A digital transactional platform enables a customer to use a device to make or receive payments and transfers and to store value electronically with a bank or non-bank permitted to store electronic value.
- Retail agents armed with a digital device connected to communications infrastructure to transmit and receive transaction details enable customers to convert cash into electronically stored value and to transform stored value back into cash. Depending on applicable regulation and the arrangement with the principal financial institution, agents may also perform other functions.

The customer device can be digital (e.g., mobile phone) that is a means of transmitting data and information or an instrument (e.g., payment card) that connects to a digital device (e.g., POS terminal). As a result of the significant advances in the accessibility and affordability provided by digital financial services, millions of poor customers are moving from exclusively cash-based transactions to formal financial services. The benefits of this development include economic growth and stability, both for the customers and for the economies where they and their families reside. However, the use of digital financial services by formerly excluded customers brings not only benefits but also risks, due in part to the characteristics of a typical poor customer (inexperienced with formal financial services and unfamiliar with consumer rights). Some of the risks are new while others, although well known, may take on different dimensions in the financial inclusion context.

This brief aims to provide national and global policy-makers with a clear picture of the rapid development of digital financial services for the poor and the need for their attention and informed understanding. It proposes a concise definition of "digital financial inclusion" and summarizes its impact on financially excluded and underserved populations; outlines the new and shifting risks of digital financial inclusion models that are significant to regulators, supervisors, and standard-setting bodies (SSBs); and concludes with observations on digital financial inclusion issues on the policy-making horizon.

"Digital financial inclusion" can be defined as digital access to and use of formal financial services by excluded and underserved populations. Such services should be suited to the customers' needs and delivered responsibly, at a cost both affordable to customers and sustainable for providers.

Today's providers of such financial services can be divided into four broad groupings based on the party holding the contractual relationship with the customer: (i) a full-service bank offering a "basic" or "simplified" transactional account for payments, transfers, and value storage via mobile device or payment card plus point-of-sale (POS) terminal; (ii) a limited-service niche bank offering such an account via mobile device or payment card plus POS terminal; (iii) a mobile network operator (MNO) e-money issuer; and (iv) a nonbank non-MNO e-money issuer. All four models function via three components: a digital transactional platform, an agent network, and the customer's access device. With these components in place, payments and transfers, as well as credit, savings, insurance, and even securities, can be offered digitally to excluded and underserved customers.

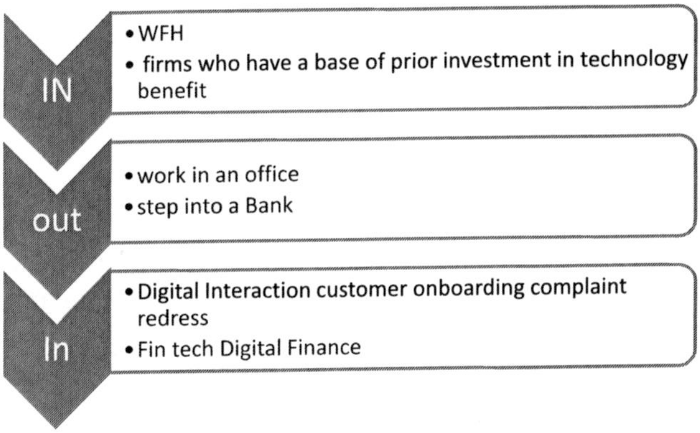

- The central bank of any country is usually the driving force in the development of national payment systems. The Reserve Bank of India as the central bank of India has been playing this developmental role and has taken several initiatives for Safe, Secure, Sound, Efficient, Accessible and Authorised payment systems in the country. The Board for Regulation and Supervision of Payment and Settlement Systems (BPSS), a sub-committee of the Central Board of the Reserve Bank of India is the highest policy making body on payment systems in the country. The BPSS is empowered for authorising, prescribing policies and setting standards for regulating and supervising all the payment and settlement systems in the country. The Department of Payment and Settlement Systems of the Reserve Bank of India serves as the Secretariat to the Board and executes its directions. In India, the payment and settlement systems are regulated by the Payment and Settlement Systems Act, 2007 (PSS Act) which was legislated in December 2007. The PSS Act as well as the Payment and Settlement System Regulations, 2008 framed thereunder came into effect from August 12, 2008. In terms of Section 4 of the PSS Act, no person other than the Reserve Bank of India (RBI) can commence or operate a payment system in India unless authorised by RBI. The Reserve Bank has since authorised payment system operators of pre-paid payment instruments, card schemes, cross-border in-bound money transfers, Automated Teller Machine (ATM) networks and centralised clearing arrangements.

Payment System Initiatives

- The Reserve Bank has taken many initiatives towards introducing and upgrading safe and efficient modes of payment systems in the country to meet the requirements of the public at large. The dominant features of large geographic spread of the country and the vast network of branches of the Indian banking system require the logistics of collection and delivery of paper instruments. These aspects of the banking structure in the country have always been kept in mind while developing the payment systems.
- At present, there are payments in India can be made through **paper based instruments**, **electronic instruments** and **other instruments**, such as, pre-paid systems, mobile banking, ATM based, Point-of-sale terminals, online transactions.

Paper-based Payments

- Use of paper-based instruments (like cheques, drafts, and the like) accounts for nearly 60% of the volume of total non-cash transactions in the country. In value terms, the share is presently around 11%. This share has been steadily decreasing over a period of time and electronic mode gained popularity due to the concerted efforts of the Reserve Bank of India to popularize the electronic payment products in preference to cash and cheques.

- Since paper based payments occupy an important place in the country, Reserve Bank had introduced Magnetic Ink Character Recognition (MICR) technology for speeding up and bringing in efficiency in processing of cheques.
- Later, a separate High Value Clearing was introduced for clearing cheques of value Rupees one lakh and above. This clearing was available at select large centres in the country (since discontinued). Recent developments in paper-based instruments include launch of Speed Clearing (for local clearance of outstation cheques drawn on core-banking enabled branches of banks), introduction of cheque truncation (CTS) system (to restrict physical movement of cheques and enable use of images for payment processing), framing CTS-2010 Standards (for enhancing the security features on cheque forms) and the like.
- While the overall thrust is to reduce the use of paper for transactions, given the fact that it would take some time to completely move to the electronic mode, the intention is to reduce the movement of paper – both for local and outstation clearance of cheques.

Electronic Payments

- The initiatives taken by the Reserve Bank in the mid-eighties and early-nineties focused on technology-based solutions for the improvement of the payment and settlement system infrastructure, coupled with the introduction of new payment products by taking advantage of the technological advancements in banks. The continued increase in the volume of cheques added pressure on the existing set-up, thus necessitating a cost-effective alternative system.

Electronic Clearing Service (ECS) Credit

- The Reserve Bank introduced the ECS (Credit) scheme during the 1990s to handle bulk and repetitive payment requirements (like salary, interest, dividend payments) of corporates and other institutions. ECS (Credit) facilitates customer accounts to be credited on the specified value date and is presently available at all major cities in the country.

- During September 2008, the Bank launched a new service known as National Electronic Clearing Service (NECS), at National Clearing Cell (NCC), Mumbai. NECS (Credit) facilitates multiple credits to beneficiary accounts with destination branches across the country against a single debit of the account of the sponsor bank. The system has a pan-India characteristic and leverages on Core Banking Solutions (CBS) of member banks, facilitating all CBS bank branches to participate in the system, irrespective of their location across the country.

Regional ECS (RECS)

- Next to NECS, RECS has been launched during the year 2009. RECS, a miniature of the NECS is confined to the bank branches within the jurisdiction of a Regional Office of RBI. Under the system, the sponsor bank will upload the validated data through the Secured Web Server of RBI containing credit/debit instructions to the customers of CBS enabled bank branches spread across the Jurisdiction of the Regional office of RBI. The RECS centre will process the data, arrive at the settlement, generate destination bank-wise data/reports and make available the data/reports through secured web-server to facilitate the destination bank branches to afford credit/debit to the accounts of beneficiaries by leveraging the CBS technology put in place by the bank. Presently RECS is available in Ahmedabad, Bengaluru, Chennai and Kolkata.

Electronic Clearing Service (ECS) Debit

- The ECS (Debit) Scheme was introduced by RBI to provide a faster method of effecting periodic and repetitive collections of utility companies. ECS (Debit) facilitates consumers / subscribers of utility companies to make routine and repetitive payments by 'mandating' bank branches to debit their accounts and pass on the money to the companies. This tremendously minimises use of paper instruments apart from improving process efficiency and customer satisfaction. There is no limit as to the minimum or maximum amount of payment. This is also available across major cities in the country.

Electronic Funds Transfer (EFT)

- This retail funds transfer system introduced in the late 1990s enabled an account holder of a bank to electronically transfer funds to another account holder with any other participating bank. Available across 15 major centers in the country, this system is no longer available for use by the general public, for whose benefit a feature-rich and more efficient system is now in place, which is the National Electronic Funds Transfer (NEFT) system.

National Electronic Funds Transfer (NEFT) System

- In November 2005, a more secure system was introduced for facilitating one-to-one funds transfer requirements of individuals / corporates. Available across a longer time window, the NEFT system provides for batch settlements at hourly intervals, thus enabling near real-time transfer of funds. Certain other unique features viz. accepting cash for originating transactions, initiating transfer requests without any minimum or maximum amount limitations, facilitating one-way transfers to Nepal, receiving confirmation of the date / time of credit to the account of the beneficiaries, etc., are available in the system.

Real Time Gross Settlement (RTGS) System

- RTGS is a funds transfer systems where transfer of money takes place from one bank to another on a "real time" and on "gross" basis. Settlement in "real time" means payment transaction is not subjected to any waiting period. "Gross settlement" means the transaction is settled on one to one basis without bunching or netting with any other transaction. Once processed, payments are final and irrevocable. This was introduced in 2004 and settles all inter-bank payments and customer transactions above ₹ 2 lakh.

Clearing Corporation of India Limited (CCIL)

- CCIL was set up in April 2001 by banks, financial institutions and primary dealers, to function as an industry service organisation for clearing and settlement of trades in money market, government securities and foreign exchange markets.

- The Clearing Corporation plays the crucial role of a Central Counter Party (CCP) in the government securities, USD – INR forex exchange (both spot and forward segments) and Collaterised Borrowing and Lending Obligation (CBLO) markets. CCIL plays the role of a central counterparty whereby, the contract between buyer and seller gets replaced by two new contracts - between CCIL and each of the two parties. This process is known as 'Novation'. Through novation, the counterparty credit risk between the buyer and seller is eliminated with CCIL subsuming all counterparty and credit risks. In order to minimize these risks, that it exposes itself to, CCIL follows specific risk management practices which are as per international best practices. In addition to the guaranteed settlement, CCIL also provides non-guaranteed settlement services for National Financial Switch (Inter bank ATM transactions) and for rupee derivatives such as Interest Rate Swaps.
- CCIL is also providing a reporting platform and acts as a repository for Over the Counter (OTC) products.

Pre-paid Payment Systems

- Pre-paid instruments are payment instruments that facilitate purchase of goods and services against the value stored on these instruments. The value stored on such instruments represents the value paid for by the holders by cash, by debit to a bank account, or by credit card. The pre-paid payment instruments can be issued in the form of smart cards, magnetic stripe cards, internet accounts, internet wallets, mobile accounts, mobile wallets, paper vouchers, etc.
- Subsequent to the notification of the PSS Act, policy guidelines for issuance and operation of prepaid instruments in India were issued in the public interest to regulate the issue of prepaid payment instruments in the country.
- The use of pre-paid payment instruments for cross-border transactions has not been permitted, except for the payment instruments approved under Foreign Exchange Management Act,1999 (FEMA).

Mobile Banking System

- Mobile phones as a medium for providing banking services have been attaining increased importance. Reserve Bank brought out a set of operating guidelines on mobile banking for banks in October 2008, according to which only banks which are licensed and supervised in India and have a physical presence in India are permitted to offer mobile banking after obtaining necessary permission from Reserve Bank. The guidelines focus on systems for security and inter-bank transfer arrangements through Reserve Bank's authorized systems. On the technology front the objective is to enable the development of inter-operable standards so as to facilitate funds transfer from one account to any other account in the same or any other bank on a real time basis irrespective of the mobile network a customer has subscribed to.

ATMs / Point of Sale (POS) Terminals / Online Transactions

- Presently, there are over 61,000 ATMs in India. Savings Bank customers can withdraw cash from any bank terminal up to 5 times in a month without being charged for the same. To address the customer service issues arising out of failed ATM transactions where the customer's account gets debited without actual disbursal of cash, the Reserve Bank has mandated re-crediting of such failed transactions within 12 working day and mandated compensation for delays beyond the stipulated period. Furthermore, a standardised template has been prescribed for displaying at all ATM locations to facilitate lodging of complaints by customers.
- There are over five lakh POS terminals in the country, which enable customers to make payments for purchases of goods and services by means of credit/debit cards. To facilitate customer convenience the Bank has also permitted cash withdrawal using debit cards issued by the banks at PoS terminals.
- The PoS for accepting card payments also include online payment gateways. This facility is used for enabling online payments for goods and services. The online payment are enabled through own payment gateways or third party service

providers called intermediaries. In payment transactions involving intermediaries, these intermediaries act as the initial recipient of payments and distribute the payment to merchants. In such transactions, the customers are exposed to the uncertainty of payment as most merchants treat the payments as final on receipt from the intermediaries. In this regard safeguard the interests of customers and to ensure that the payments made by them using Electronic/Online Payment modes are duly accounted for by intermediaries receiving such payments, directions were issued in November 2009. Directions require that the funds received from customers for such transactions need to be maintained in an internal account of a bank and the intermediary should not have access to the same.

- Further, to reduce the risks arising out of the use of credit/ debit cards over internet/IVR (technically referred to as card not present (CNP) transactions), Reserve Bank mandated that all CNP transactions should be additionally authenticated based on information not available on the card and an online alert should be sent to the cardholders for such transactions.

Oversight of Payment and Settlement Systems

Oversight of the payment and settlement systems is a central bank function whereby the objectives of safety and efficiency are promoted by monitoring existing and planned systems, assessing them against these objectives and, where necessary, inducing change. By overseeing payment and settlement systems, central banks help to maintain systemic stability and reduce systemic risk, and to maintain public confidence in payment and settlement systems. The Payment and Settlement Systems Act, 2007 and the Payment and Settlement Systems Regulations, 2008 framed thereunder, provide the necessary statutory backing to the Reserve Bank of India for undertaking the Oversight function over the payment and settlement systems in the country.

What is happening?

New digital transactional platforms – such as bKash in Bangladesh, which reached nearly a quarter of the country's adult population of over 160 million in its first two years – offer convenient and vastly less expensive ways to make payments and transfer funds. In addition, these platforms can offer a safe place to store value for hundreds of millions of households that rely on the proverbial mattress. These platforms accommodate the very small and unpredictable cash flows of the poor, allowing them to transact affordably in tiny amounts whenever they wish, subject to the vagaries of sometimes unpredictable or unreliable connections and other risks.

Digital transactional platforms yield further benefits for financial inclusion by providing both a means to access additional financial services, such as interest-bearing savings, credit, insurance, and even investment products. They also generate data that financial providers can use to design financial products tailored to the repayment capacity and financial needs of the specific poor and low-income customer segments.

The dramatic rate at which poor consumers are taking up products, such as the one-month M-Shwari consumer loans offered by Commercial Bank of Africa (CBA) to M-Pesa customers in Kenya or the life insurance products marketed to Tigo (Ghana) mobile phone pre-paid customers, speaks volumes about demand. One million M-Shwari loans were issued within 41 days of the product's launch, catapulting CBA from a modestly sized corporate lender to one of the largest retail players in Kenyan banking. Tigo's Family Care life insurance product doubled the insurance market in Ghana in its first year of operation. With the advent of ever cheaper smartphones, the pace of change will only accelerate.

What is changing with digital financial inclusion and what is on the horizon for policy makers?

Digital financial inclusion introduces new market participants and allocates roles and risks (both new and well-known) in different ways compared to traditional approaches to retail financial service delivery. The three key components of digital financial inclusion models correspond to the three main triggers of new or shifting risks:

- The **new parties** and arrangements involved in the digital transactional platform, and specifically in the management and storage of account data and the holding of customer funds;

- The **technology** used by the device and the digital transactional platform; and
- The **use of agents** as the principal customer interface.

These triggers, as well as the typical profile of the financially excluded or underserved customers in question, introduce operational risks, consumer-related risks, and financial crime risks, among others. Understanding and mitigating these risks will be key to achieving the game-changing potential rewards of digital financial inclusion.

Increasing numbers of countries worldwide are putting in place regulatory regimes that allow more poor people to access and use basic formal financial services they need to improve their lives. The Financial Action Task Force (FATF), which sets international standards for anti-money laundering and countering the financing of terrorism (AML/CFT), has taken significant action over the past two years, making it easier for policy-makers to pursue financial inclusion goals while combating money laundering, terrorist financing, and other financial crimes.

Current regulatory trends reflect steadily growing awareness among FATF members over the past decade that country-level implementation of FATF's AML/CFT standards and guidance can inadvertently prevent poor households and businesses from accessing formal financial services (or discourage their use even where there is access). The financial exclusion that results can compromise countries' ability to track money laundering and terrorist financing by relegating vast numbers of people and transactions to the untraceable world of cash. This culminated in FATF's formal recognition of financial exclusion as a money laundering and terrorist financing risk as reflected in the FATF Ministers' approval of the organization's 2012–2020 mandate. Financial inclusion and AML/CFT are now recognized as mutually supportive and complementary objectives: the application of measures that enable more citizens to use formal financial services will increase the reach and effectiveness of AML/CFT regimes.

This formal recognition coincides with significant FATF actions of relevance to financial inclusion taken in the past two years:

- FATF's Forty Recommendations on AML/CFT—the body's highest level normative pronouncements on the subject for countries to follow in crafting their domestic AML/CFT regimes—were revised to introduce the requirement of national and sectoral risk assessments, embedding a "risk-based approach" (RBA) to AML/CFT regulation and supervision, and expanding on the concepts of "lower risk" and "low risk" activities.
- FATF released updated guidance on Anti-Money Laundering and Terrorist Financing Measures and Financial Inclusion produced jointly with the World Bank and the Asia/Pacific Group on Money-Laundering, and new guidance was issued on Prepaid Cards, Mobile Payments and Internet Based Payment Services.
- FATF revised the Assessment Methodology used to assess a country's compliance with the FATF Recommendations (which are vitally important in determining which countries get added to or removed from public lists FATF maintains of noncompliant jurisdictions), incorporating for the first time assessment of the effectiveness of a given country's AML/CFT regime, and explicitly including financial exclusion and financial inclusion policies as factors that assessors may consider in their evaluations.

Collectively, these actions clarify the landscape for country-level policy making, offering new opportunities—in some cases, even incentives—for policy-makers to adopt inclusion-friendly AML/CFT regimes.

Digital Financial Inclusion is the way forward

Covid –has brought this out clearly and powerfully and India is making all attempts to ensure digital financial inclusion.

Chapter - VIII

Policy Choices in the Pandemic

"It was the best of times, it was the worst of times, it was the age of wisdom, it was the age of foolishness, it was the epoch of belief, it was the epoch of incredulity, it was the season of Light, it was the season of Darkness, it was the spring of hope, it was the winter of despair, we had everything before us, we had nothing before us, we were all going direct to Heaven, we were all going direct the other way - in short, the period was so like the present **period, that some of its noisiest authorities insisted on its being received, for good or for evil, in the superlative degree of comparison only." Charles Dickens: A Tale of Two Cities.**

Covid-19 is the black swan event that is impacting most of our established practices, norms and regulations, and thus shaping to become the big Disruptor the economic loss from the Pandemic will be immense but cannot yet be quantified as we are in the midst of it. This downturn has caused widespread anxiety about the imminence of a recession with the fear that the world may have been derailed from a high growth trajectory.

There are many parallels drawn between 2008 and 2020. While 2008 was more a financial sector problem spilling over to the real sector, this time it is a real sector problem which is being addressed through financial sector. This may be a necessary condition but not a sufficient one to bring the economy back on track.

The Pandemic has starkly shown us our challenges and the weak spots in our Economy. Poor Infrastructure, Weak and excessive regulation, small manufacturing sector, no social safety nets and a workforce with inadequate education, skills, and a lack of overall governance.

1. India needs to create jobs and employment to harness the skills of its young population. If this is not done with immediacy the demographic bonus will not be harnessed. Economic Disparities are widening. Access to TV and social media leads to aspiration for higher standards of living. If this rising aspiration is not met. As the gap between the Haves and the Have notes widens it is not a good portent. If this revolution of rising expectations which is growing in society. If it is not translated to an ability to achieve it through employment, jobs, and a regular income stream, it will further widen the disparities in society and youth will turn to lawlessness and crime.
2. To focus on the creation of world class Infrastructure which will have a multiplier effect in terms of job creation. Infrastructure deficit is a serious shortfall which hampers and trammels the processes of economic growth. It is imperative to increase the coverage to reach the most remote and least developed areas by widening infrastructure.
3. Enhanced investments in manufacturing is essential.
4. Divert the large proportion of population engaged in subsistence agriculture into the high value addition jobs created by investments in manufacturing.
5. A skill and effective capacity building programme is required to build the necessary capabilities for integration with the emerging job market.
6. We should increase the pace of digitization. Digitisation has proved its effectiveness during the course of the Pandemic. It has created efficiencies in delivery of goods and services and needs to be widened and deepened. The trilogy of the Jan-Dhan-Aadhar-Mobile has enabled benefits to percolate to the poor while excluding the better off it has allowed for,

lowering transaction costs and reduced leakages with effective targeting this needs to be scaled up for more efficient delivery of services.

7. The Pandemic has thrown up the need to address the Public Health challenge.
8. The need to build social safety nets for the poor to ensure inclusive growth while maintaining macroeconomic stability has been starkly brought out by the mass migration of the poor migrants from the big cities back to their village homes in the rural hinterland which they fled due to the absence of livelihood opportunities in the villages.
9. The central bank is clearly no longer the only game in town at the same time its role should not be taken lightly either's role should not be underestimated. Monetary policy, liquidity management, financial regulation and supervision are very blunt instruments tools but they can still moderate economic and financial conditions.
10. The financial sector plays a critical role in the Indian Economy. Its role gains even greater salience in aiding the resumption of economic activity and helping to find a way out of the dire straits we find ourselves mired in. Financial Institutions, instruments and markets which comprise the financial sector act as a conduit for the transfer of financial resources from net savers to net borrowers. Institutionalisation of savings and investments leads to augmentation of savings and more judicious allocation of resources. The gain to the economy will depend largely on how efficiently the financial sector performs the basic function of intermediation.
11. The Banking Sector in the Covid-19 Pandemic has to follow a Supply leading approach. Much has been done to improve the financial sector soundness and depth much more needs to be done to improve the efficiency with which financial resources are allocated to finance the higher levels of investment necessary for sustained growth and poverty reduction.

In the backdrop of the uncertainties of global economic revival created by the Covid-19 Pandemic, and as risks become more difficult to anticipate and manage. As the fears of global recession and the raging pandemic hobble us.

We are confronted by three urgent macroeconomic challenges in managing the Pandemic and the recovery.

1. Managing the Growth Inflation Dynamic
2. Mitigating the vulnerability of the external sector
3. Managing the fall out of Fiscal expansionism.

That said, we are dealing with a pandemic superimposed on a slowdown. The response has to be a coordinated one, with all arms of public policy as well as other stakeholders in the economy pulling together and working in close cooperation. Obviously, the government has a very important role in the response to the crisis.

The Way Forward

Jerome Powell the chair of the Federal Reserve has best expressed it "No one has the luxury of choosing their challenges Fate and History provide them for us. We entered this crisis on a solid economic foundation and will build a bridge to a position of regained economic strength on the other side"

The crisis highlights the need for urgent action to cushion the recovery from the pandemic's health and economic consequences, protect vulnerable populations, may we never see images of helpless hopeless migrants trekking to their homes in despair see loss of lives and livelihoods. May the recovery and the economic rebound set the stage for a lasting economic growth trajectory which promises growth with equity. Only the realization of that promise will make India a truly great Nation.

What has the Pandemic changed forever ? The Pandemic has fundamentally altered the way we live, think, and work.

Work From Home

Lets take work first, Work from home has become the new norm. WFH is here to stay what are its upsides, we feel less exhausted and more productive, we spend less time in the grinding commute. We have more time for family. On the downside we are in a state of anomie and alienation, we fell caged cabined cribbed in and confined. There is no one at our elbow to help us out. We miss the coffee break, the grapevine, the cooler room chat with our colleagues. We also have to cope with the demands of housework and home which seem to multiply for women where care burden has increased and there is no outlet no escape from the home or the overwhelming need sometimes, to just be by oneself. It is about public and private spaces that both Katherine Mansfield and Virginia Woolf, long ago so powerfully evoked.

Social Interaction & Official Meetings Annual General Meetings

Weddings, and life events, birthdays and anniversaries are now celebrated with the family meeting over a zoom call. Official Meetings can be held over a phone with a video chat and Companies are now holding shareholder meetings including the sacrosanct Annual General Meeting with e-ballots and proper voting over the internet.

Media Usage

There has been an explosion in Media usage, the sixty and staid only used the T.V. to watch the 9 o'clock English news, now everybody and his dog enjoy Netflix and hours are spent on the Internet. We rise and shine with the digital downloaded newspaper. We connect with friends and family on social media. All the Drivers, Maids, Mails, Dhobis everyone has a phone and is on WhatsApp. We have started doing housework on our own. Microwave ovens and Dishwashers are flying off the shelf we need speed and convenience, we have discovered new ways of cooking, microwave is no longer just used for warming food. The market for e-groceries and prepackaged food instant food, has also grown. TV dinners are fast becoming a new normal.

Education

Children have online classes, teenagers have online tuition and those studying for the competitive examinations have online coaching.

They have study groups and play groups with special planned leisure games.

New Sunrise Sectors

Old sectors as Automobiles, Aviation, Services, Hospitality, Hotels have slowed there are no conferences, or large meets hotel ballrooms are deserted but new sectors have come up Pharma of course is big ticket, as is research and development as the whole world awaits a vaccine.

Connectivity Enabled Growth

There has been an exponential connectivity enabled growth in sectors like e-commerce, in online shopping, online grocery and food delivery.

Banking

Banking has changed fundamentally as e-banking has increased, online payment platforms, loan platforms, crowd sourced loans, are also creating disintermediation and competition for the banks.

Central Banking

Even staid central banks have changed they have recognised albeit reluctantly digital currency and are even considering digital currency as a reserve asset.

Payment Systems

There has been an impetus to growth in speedier payment systems and the RBI has green flagged the setting up of a new umbrella organisation for payment aggregators. The payment and settlement systems recorded a robust growth during 2019-20, growing by 44.1 percent in terms of volume on top of the expansion by 55.8 percent in the previous year. In terms of value, it increased by 5.4 percent on top of 14.2 percent in the previous year, mainly due to lower growth observed in the large value system, viz., Real Time Gross Settlement (RTGS) system. The share of digital transactions in the total volume of non-cash retail payments increased to 97.0 percent during 2019-20, up from 95.4 percent in the previous year. However, the extended period of lockdown arising on account of the COVID-19 pandemic resulted in subdued economic activity and lower discretionary payments, thereby leading to a fall in digital transactions.

NEFT National Electronic Fund Transfers are now free and are also available 24×7, round the clock.

Pandemic Planning and Monitoring

Pandemic monitoring and planning a response has been aided by Apps like the Arogya Setu, surveillance, testing, contact monitoring has been facilitated through these digital APS.

Medicine

Telemedicine has seen an increase and online consultation with Doctors has increased.

Inflection Point

There is an inflection point for increase in technology the way we see the world and the ability to realize the Digital Mission.

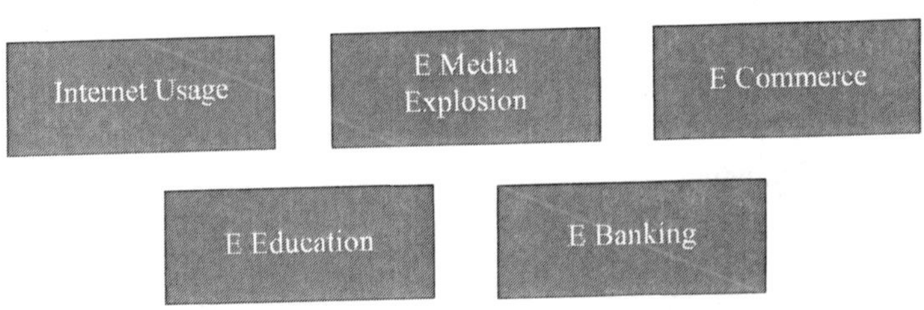

This brings us to the increased fear of the deepening Digital Divide and digital apartheid. Digital financial inclusion pushes the excluded sections of society further into the margins of society. It is absolutely necessary to mainstream the marginalised Dalits, poor women scheduled castes and tribes, illiterate or digitally non-literate, the unserved and underserved, so that through the processes of formalisation they are plugged into the mother lode of the formal economy as producers and consumers of goods and services.

Understanding Exclusion

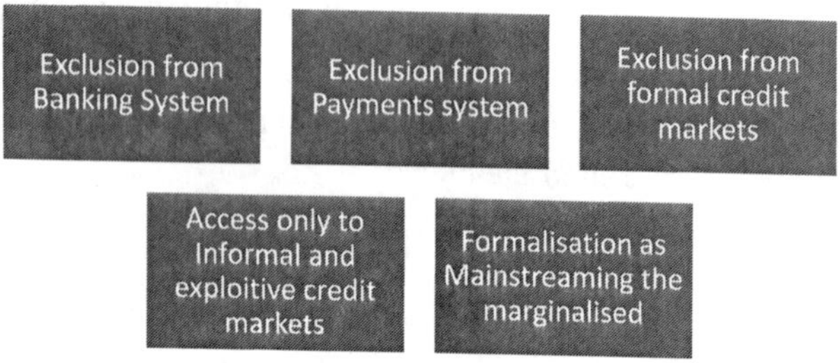

How is this to be viewed. Those who lack access to the Banking Systems, though as the Aadhar Card enables quicker opening of zero balance Jan Dhan accounts and as several welfare measures for the poor are being delivered through the Jan Dhan accounts as financial support of Rs 500 delivered to women holders of Jan Dhan accounts etc. there has been a rush for getting Jan Dhan accounts in the Pandemic. Exclusion from a banking system also excludes them from the payment system, which means that if money has to be sent to the village from the big city it becomes a long, arduous and costly affair to send it through a human courier, while having a bank account makes this almost costless and money can be sent by the migrant worker with speed and efficiency to his family. Likewise it leads to an exclusion from the formal credit markets and a recourse to informal and exploitive informal credit markets, a bank enables savings credit, remittances, Insurance, Pension, and payment transactions this is the way we must SRIPT Inclusion.

Factors Which Need to be Surmounted to Ensure Inclusion

We have seen the need for Inclusion and understood its benefits, let us understand the barriers to this process.

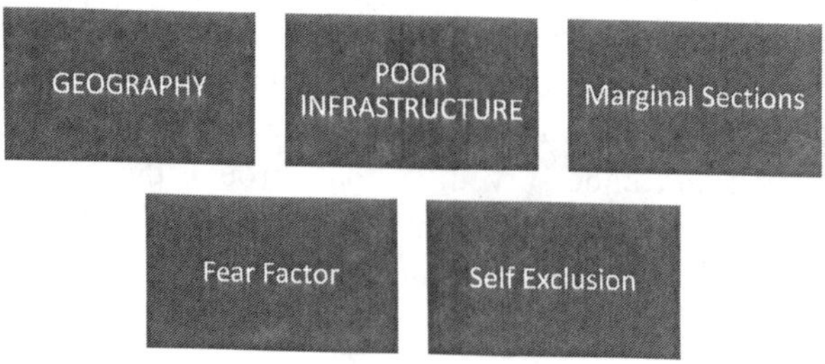

The infrastructure is very poor even today we have one bank branch per 14000 people one Business correspondent serves six or seven if not more villages. There are also barriers of geography in our country of sub-continental proportions. We have hill regions which are difficult to reach where people are few and spread out urban areas where people jostle for space, coastal areas, desert areas, there is no uniform solution possible in a country of sub-continental propositions. We need to devise bespoke solutions for each area.

Marginalised sectors, are the totally unserved populations the weaker sections which are outside the formal financial system, the dalits, the scheduled castes and tribes and the poorer vulnerable sections.

These illiterate and unserved sections are seized by the fear factor, they are afraid of endless paperwork they do not understand technology the leitmotif of their lives is fear it governs all their actions and reactions, they need a great deal of handholding and capacity building. They have a threat perception from formal institutional structures they obtain services at much higher, usurious costs.

SELF EXCLUSION is the greatest barrier which needs to be overcome. The pandemic has shown us clearly that economic growth without equity is a travesty. This will lead to greater difficulty and to sharper and more dangerous divisions in society if we don't watch out. Today the migrants accept their fate and peacefully trudge homeward from the inhospitable, and pitiless city, tomorrow they may revolt and loot and pillage if the state does not step in swiftly to address these growing economic disparities.

Environmental Consiousness

The pandemic has shown us that the resources of the planet are not infinite, we must reduce the carbon footprint, focus on climate change, the pandemic is increasing global consciousness for environmentally sustainable growth.

New Economic Paradigm

The world has seen fundamental changes to which India must now adapt. We have a demographic bonus of a large and young population, a working age population which can power domestic growth we can produce and consume on our own. What we need are jobs to harness the skills and potential of our young people to make them earning members, savers and consumers of goods and services to ratchet up our Economic Growth in the years ahead as we look forward to a leadership role in the comity of nations.

Index

A

Aadhar Card, 198
Aadhar enabled bank account, 170
Aadhar-enabled payment system, 170
Account Aggregators, 93
Additional chunk of imports, 102
Additional risk premium, 79
Administrative reforms, 56
Advanced economies, 29
Advantages of Consolidation, 107
Advisory Committee, 48
Agricultural credit, 150
Agricultural exports, 152
Agricultural Produce Market Committee, 159
Agricultural Produce Marketing Committee Mandis, 65
Agriculture sector domestic markets, 37
Ahmedabad, 182
Allahabad Bank, 117, 118, 124
Andhra Pradesh, 168
Anti-Money Laundering, 189
Antonio Gutteras, 25
Arogya Setu, 197
Artificial Intelligence, 75, 116
Asia Pacific Region, 27
Asia-Pacific, 26
Assessment Methodology, 189
Asset Reconstruction Fund, 122
Atma Nirbhar, 44
Atma Nirbhar Bharat Abhiyan, 82
Atma Nirbhar Bharat Package, 53, 102, 105, 113, 151
Atmanirbhar Bharat, 64, 106
Atmanirbhar Bharat Yojna, 73
Automated Teller Machine, 168, 180
Automation sector, 35
Aviation sector, 34
AXIS Bank, 120
Azim Premji Trust, 120

B

Backward and forward linkages, 86
Backwardness Trap, 72
Balance sheet, 79
Bangladesh, 186
Bank Board Bureau, 124
Bank Boards, 125
Bank Capital, 122
Bank charges, 61
Bank for International Settlements, 114
Bank Investment Company, 124
Bank mergers, 122
Bank Nationalisation Act, 123

Bank of America, 28
Bank of Baroda, 107, 117
Bank of India, 107
Bank of International Settlements, 28
Bank of Rajasthan, 108, 121
Bank officials, 78
Bank ownership, 123
Bank shareholders, 129
Bank Solvency, 122
Banking Regulation Act, 115, 123
Banking Sector, 193
Banking Sector reforms, 121
Banking System, 12, 112
Bankruptcy Board of India, 132
Bankruptcy Code, 89
Banks Asset Quality risk, 34
Banks Balance Sheets, 118
Banks Investors, 39
Basle Committee, 122
Benares State Bank Ltd, 107
Bengaluru, 182
Bharatmala, 76
Bihar, 125
Black Swan, 44
Board for Industrial and Financial Reconstruction, 140
Board Level Decisions, 118
Board Level leadership, 118
Borrowing limits for States, 62
Bottlenecks and Major Challenges, 172
Brahmanical structure, 107
Branch Expansion Policy, 122
Brazil, 29
Break in Consumer Spending, 25
Budget estimate, 57
Budgeted Expenditure, 59

C

Capital Adequacy Ratio, 123
Capital Conservation Buffers, 118
Capital Expenditure, 60, 62
Capital Markets, 118
Casualisation of Employment, 173
Central Asia, 22
Central Bank, 43
Central bank of any country, 179
Central Bank of India, 124
Central Banking, 196
Central Bureau of Investigation, 124
Central Counter Party, 183
Central Public Works Dept, 55
Central Statistics Office, 84
Central Vigilance Commission, 124
Centurion Bank Ltd, 107, 108
Centurion Bank of Punjab Ltd, 108
Ceramics, 98
Challenges Faced by Banks, 74
Challenges in Agriculture Financing, 154
Chennai, 137, 182
China, 33
Chinese imports, 43
Christine Lagarde, 26
Claudio Borio, 28
Clearing Corporation of India Limited, 183
Climate Change, 22
Cluster Administrative Authorities, 76
Cluster development, 80
Cluster Manufacturing, 76
Collapse in capital goods production, 39
Combined Fiscal Deficit, 62
Commercial Bank of Africa, 187
Commercial paper, 49

Commercial vehicle sales, 40
Connectivity Enabled Growth, 196
Constraints on modernisation and expansions, 86
Consumer Price Index, 48
Contours of response, 53
Contract farming, 65
Contract Farming Ordinance, 151
Cooperative Banking System, 114
Cooperative Banks, 115
Core Banking Solutions, 116, 182
Corporate Debt Restructuring, 130
Corporate Governance, 139
Corporate risk, 34
Corporation Bank, 118, 124
Counter-cyclical capital buffer, 47
Coverage Ratio, 109
Credit cards, 170
Credit demand, 127
Credit facilities, 168
Credit facility, 78
Credit Guarantee, 83
Credit Guarantee Scheme banks, 78
Credit Guarantee Trust, 60
Credit Guarantee Trust Fund, 80
Credit Risk Evaluation, 38
Crypto Currency, 145
Current Account Convertibility, 122
Cyber incident, 112

D

Dairy and dairy supplements, 98
Data Analysis, 112
Data Analytics, 75
Debit cards, 170
Debt Recovery Tribunal, 122, 132, 134
Defence production, 57
Delayed Payments, 87
Deleveraging China, 22
Demographic Factors, 100
Dena Bank, 117
Devouring forest fire, 11
Diamonds and precious stones, 46
Digital Delivery Post Covid Response, 113
Digital financial inclusion, 164, 178, 187
Digital financial services, 163
Digital Mission, 197
Digital transactional platforms, 187
Digitisation of land records, 155
Direct Benefit Transfer, 165
Direct Benefit transfers, 65
Direct credit programmes, 66
Domestic air passenger traffic, 40
Domestic growth, 35
Domestic Vulnerabilities, 36

E

Economic and financial activity, 51
Economic Prosperity, 13
Economic Recovery, 25, 39, 63
Economic Survey, 149
Efficient and high-quality production, 96
Effluent discharge norms, 97
Elastic Run, 157
Electricity consumption, 39
Electronic Funds Transfer, 182
Electronic National Agriculture Markets, 151
Emergency Credit Line Guarantee Scheme, 89
Emerging market economies, 29
Employment generation for Tribals, 55
Employment Opportunities, 72

Enforce accountability, 131
Entertainment sector, 34
Essential Commodities Act, 56, 65, 152
Europe, 22
European Business Leaders' Convention, 26
European Central Bank, 26
Exclusion of First Time Borrowers, 71
Exim Bank of India, 46
Expert Committee on MSMEs, 90
Export Credit, 46
Export sector, 101
Extension of Time, 46
External Benchmark for MSME Loans, 92
External Sector, 49

F

Factory output, 25
Factory output data, 127
Farm produce, 158
Farm Tele Advisors, 158
Farmer Producer Organisations, 158
Farmer Producers Organisations, 156
Farmers' Produce Trade and Commerce, 152
Federal Bank, 108
Federal Bank Ltd, 108
Finance Minister, 54
Financial Action Task Force, 188
Financial Frauds, 144
Financial Inclusion Survey Report, 154
Financial institutions, 163, 174
Financial sector, 44
Financial Services Providers, 140
Financial Stability, 105
FinTech companies, 93, 113
FinTech firms, 113
Fiscal deficit target, 63
Fiscal expansionism, 194
Fiscal Year, 38
Food and Agricultural Organisation, 160
Food processing, 152
Forecast of a normal monsoon, 50
Foreign Currency Inflows, 40, 49
Foreign Exchange Reserves, 50
Foreign tourist arrivals halted, 40
Foreign Trade Policy, 60
Full-service bank, 178

G

Ganesh Bank, 107
Gender and Exclusion, 173
Gender and the Pandemic, 24
General credit cards, 170
Global Economic Prospects Report, 23
Global Findex database, 173
Global Findex Report, 167
Global Pandemic corona virus, 21
Global Partnership, 172
Global prices, 50
Global Ratings, 27
Global Supply Chain, 102
Global Supply Chains and Technology, 24
Global Trust Bank, 107, 121
Global Value Chains, 94
Global winds, 11
Goldman Sachs, 28
Great Depression, 38
Gross Financial Assets, 126
Gross Value Added, 149, 152
Groundwater tables, 161
Growth Inflation Dynamic, 194

H

Haryana, 168
HDFC Bank, 108
Health Package, 64
High cost structure, 99
High frequency indicators, 40
High Value Clearing, 181
Higher premium, 79
Himachal Pradesh, 168
Housing Finance Companies, 106, 141
Housing sector, 55

I

Immediate Payment Service, 114
Implementation of Interest Subvention Scheme, 153
Importance of Institutional Credit, 150
Imports from China, 102
Improving credit risk management, 130
Income Tax Department, 172
Income Tax department, 171
Income tax returns, 171
Income Taxes, 61
Index on Financial Inclusion, 168
India Ratings and Research, 109
India-digital Payments, 114
Indian agriculture, 150
Indian Bank, 117
Indian Banking Industry, 123
Indian Bankruptcy Code, 58
Indian Banks, 37
Indian Banks Association, 139
Indian Economy, 42
Indian exports, 85
Indian Financial System, 106
India's Financial Sector, 106
Industrial corridors, 76
Industrial Development Bank Ltd, 108
Industrial Production, 25
Industrial raw materials, 50
Ineffective marketing strategy, 85
Inflation Target, 48
Information Communication and Technology, 96
Information utilities, 132
Infrastructure Leasing and Finance Company, 34
Innovation Regulatory Sandbox RBI Cohorts, 94
Insolvency and Bankruptcy Board of India, 90
Insolvency and Bankruptcy Code, 37, 88, 109, 137
Insolvency Professionals, 133
Integration with Global Value Chains, 94
Interest Rate Structure, 121
Internal Working Group, 155
International Labour Organization, 173
International market, 100
International Standards, 122
International trade barriers, 99
Internet Based Payment Services, 189
Investment activity, 39
Investment Credit Rating Agency, 58

J

Jamie Caruana, 176
Jan Dhan account holders, 65
Jan Dhan accounts, 198
Jan-Dhan-Aadhar-Mobile, 192
Japan, 66
Jerome Powell, 25
Jharkhand, 125
Joint Lenders' Forum, 130

K

Karnataka, 168
Katherine Mansfield, 195
Kenya, 187
Kenyan banking, 187
Kerala, 168
Key components, 177
Keynes theory, 58
Kharif crop, 160
Kisan Call Centres, 158
Kisan Credit Cards, 156, 168
Kolkata, 137, 182
Korea, 66
Kotak Mahindra, 119
Kotak Mahindra Bank, 120
Kudremukh Iron, 61

L

Labour Market, 63
Lack of patent protection, 99
Latin America, 22
Leather and footwear, 81
Leather and Leather Products, 98
Legal Environmental Factors, 99
Less Professional management, 129
Leveraging Industrial Revolution, 76
Limited capital and knowledge, 85
Liquidity Adjustment Facility, 48
Liquidity Support, 59
Long Term Repercussions, 30
Low production capacity, 85

M

Machine Learning, 116, 143
Magnetic Ink Character Recognition, 180
Maharashtra, 62, 168
Maharashtra Cooperative Bank, 75, 115
Mandi Tax, 151
Market Characteristics, 100
Marketing support, 81
Measures to Ease Financial Stress, 46
Meat and Sea Food Exports, 98
Medicines and Spices, 98
Mega public projects, 76
Mergers of Public Sector Banks, 141
Metal products, 81
Micro Finance Institutions, 91, 154
Micro Small and Medium Enterprises, 60
Micro-Finance Institutions, 143
Migrant workers, 55
Mobile banking, 170
Mobile Banking System, 184
Mobile network operator, 165, 178
Mobile Payments, 189
Mobile wallets, 170
Monetary Policy Committee, 39
Moratorium period, 83
Mudra Shishu loans, 55
Multi State Cooperative Banks, 115
Mumbai, 137

N

Narasimham Committee, 121, 122
Narasimham Committee Report II, 122
Narasimhan Committee, 107
Narrow Banking, 123
National Agriculture Market Scheme, 153
National Clearing Cell, 181
National Company Law Tribunal, 88, 132, 134
National Credit Guarantee Trust, 66
National Electronic Clearing Service, 181

National Electronic Funds Transfer, 114, 183, 197
National Infrastructure Pipeline, 59
National level agency, 156
National lockdown, 25
National Payments Corporation of India, 114
National Sample Survey, 72
Native Art and Artefacts, 98
Need to improve Ease of Doing business, 77
Negative Economic Growth, 64
Net banking, 170
Net Financial Assets, 126
Net Stable Funding Ratio, 109
New Bank of India, 107
New Dimensions of Banking, 145
New Frontiers of Banking, 143
Nick Leeson, 107
Non Bank Finance Companies, 106, 107
Non Bank Finance Sector, 75
Non Banking Financial Companies, 71
Non Budgeted Expenditure, 59, 64
Non-availability of skilled labour, 86
Non-availability of suitable technology, 85
Non-Bank Financial Companies, 141
Non-Banking Financial Companies, 95
Non-debt capital receipts, 63
Non-Performing Assets, 110, 141
Non-performing assets, 74, 110, 138

O

Oil Market Disruptions, 22
Oil producing countries, 40
Old sectors as Automobiles, 196
One Time Restructuring, 91
Online Transactions, 185
Open Market Operation, 48
Organic Supplements and Herbs, 98
Oriental Bank of Commerce, 107, 117, 121
Outlook for the Indian Economy, 50

P

Pan-India New Umbrella Entity, 114
Pandemic Relief Measures, 77
Paper-based Payments, 180
Payment System Initiatives, 180
Performing loan losses, 129
Permanent Account Number, 166
Persistent and Perceived Barriers to Growth, 86
Personal protective equipment, 69
Petroleum Products, 98
PJ Nayak Committee, 123
Police Brutality, 23
Policy Choices and the Way Forward, 93
Political Pressure, 129
Post Covid World, 146
Post-Covid shock, 63
Post-Harvest crop, 157
Pradhan Mantri Krishi Sinchai Yojana, 153
Pre-Covid economic scenario, 42
Pre-paid instruments, 184
Prepaid Cards, 189
Prepaid instruments, 170
Priority sector categorisation, 66
Private and Public Sector Banks, 44
Private Bank, 119, 120
Private Banks, 119
Private consumption, 39
Private Sector Banks, 125, 126, 140
Problem of Scale, 76

Product quality certifications, 97
Prohibitive Cost Structures, 99
Promoting financial inclusion, 175
Prospects of Economic Recovery, 63
Public Credit Registry, 94
Public Health, 59
Public Sector Banks, 61, 62, 107, 111, 118, 119, 120, 123, 124, 125, 126
Punjab, 115, 168
Punjab National Bank, 34, 107, 117

R

Rabi Crop, 157
Rajeev Joshi, 80
Rapid technology adoption, 97
Rates of Interest, 71
Rating Agencies, 37, 39, 43
RBI Annual Report, 152
RBI Measures to Improve the Credit Flow, 91
RBIs Financial Sector Development Report, 110
Real Estate, 55
Real Time Gross Settlement, 183, 197
Reason for Giving Credit Guarantees, 74
Receivables Exchange of India Ltd., 92
Reducing Fixed Costs, 72
Reforming land lease framework, 155
Reforms in Agriculture, 63
Reforms in agriculture, 65
Regional Comprehensive Economic Partnership, 43
Regional Handicrafts, 98
Registrar of Cooperative Banks, 115
Reserve Bank, 12, 47, 48, 49, 87, 92, 140, 185, 186
Reserve Bank Accommodative Stance, 40
Reserve Bank of India, 109, 167, 179, 180
Resolving Delay in Receipt of Payments, 92
Review of banking laws, 123
Rising Social Tensions, 22
Robotics and related technologies, 75
Role of MSMEs in Indian Economy, 84
Rural Infrastructure Development Fund, 155

S

Sagarmala, 76
Sangli Bank, 108
Scheduled Commercial Banks, 137
Secure digital payments, 175
Secured Web Server, 182
Self-Help Group Bank Linkage Programme, 156
Self-Reliant India Scheme, 82
Service sector activity, 40
Settlement Systems Act, 179, 186
Shipping Corporation of India, 61
Sikkim, 168
Sikkim Bank, 107
Single window clearances, 76
Slowing Indian Economy, 42
Small and marginal farmers, 55
Small and Medium Enterprises, 96
Small Finance Banks, 95, 143
Small Industries Development Bank, 48
Smart Sampling Technique, 157
Social safety nets, 193
Soil Health Cards, 153

South Africa, 29
Special liquidity facility, 48
Standard and Poors, 36
Standard-setting bodies, 164
State Bank of India Act, 123
Statutory Auditors, 113
Stimulate consumer demand, 61
Stock market movements, 65
Street vendors, 55
Strengthening Banks in India, 122
Strengthening Regulation and Supervision, 112
Stressed Assets, 118
Strong brand names, 98
Strong Fundamentals Weakening Growth, 33
Sumerian grain trade, 111
Supply Chains, 42
Swaminathan Committee, 151

T

Tamil Nadu, 23, 168
Tax Concessions, 64
Tax deducted at source, 171
Tax Measures, 55
Technological Disruption, 75
Technology-savvy industries, 84
Temporary shortage of labour, 50
Terrorist Financing Measures, 189
Trade barriers, 100
Trade liberalisation, 98
Trade Receivable Discounting System, 61, 92, 143
Trade Tensions, 22
Trade war, 101
Traditional banks, 146
Traditional businesses, 113
Traditional public service, 169
Transin Logistics, 157
Transparency and accountability, 175
Transport & Highways, 55
Truck Guru, 157
Truck Suvidha, 157
Twin Balance Sheet problems, 35

U

Umbrella Organisation, 143
UN Secretary General, 25
Uncertain Recovery, 29
Unified Payment Interface, 114, 170
Union Bank of India, 107
Union Budget, 63
Union Budget App Based Invoice Financing, 93
United Bank of India, 117
United Nations Conference on Trade and Development, 25
United Nations World Economic Situation, 24
United States, 33
United States Economy, 25
United States Federal Reserve Chairman, 25
United Western Bank, 108, 121
Unstructured Supplementary Service Data, 170
Urban Co-operative Banks, 142
Urban Cooperative Banks, 75, 115
Urban cooperative banks, 75, 116
US dollar weakening, 30
US Rail Road Bonds, 38

V

Various schemes of mutual funds, 49
Vietnam and Bangladesh, 43

Virginia Woolf, 195
Volatile Market conditions, 118

W

Weakening Financial Sector, 36
Wood and furniture, 81
Work from home, 195
Working capital cycle, 46
World Bank, 22, 170, 172, 173, 189
World Bank's Board, 95
World Bank's Global Financial Inclusion Database, 167
World Economic Outlook, 29

Y

Yes Bank, 119, 120, 126

Z

Zero Defect, 77
Zero effect, 77